The Greatest COOKIES EVER

The Greatest COOKIES EVER

Dozens of Delicious,
Chewy, Chunky,
Fun & Foolproof
Recipes

ROSE DUNNINGTON

LARK BOOKS
A Division of Sterling Publishing Co., Inc.
New York

Editor
Veronika Alice Gunter

Art Director
Stacey Budge

**Creative Director
and Cover Designer**
Celia Naranjo

Photographer
Stewart O'Shields

Associate Art Director
Shannon Yokeley

Editorial Assistance
Delores Gosnell

Library of Congress Cataloging-in-Publication Data

Dunnington, Rose.
  The greatest cookies ever : dozens of delicious, chewy,
chunky, fun & foolproof recipes / by Rose Dunnington.
      p. cm.
  Includes index.
  ISBN 1-57990-627-3 (hardcover)
  1. Cookies. I. Title.
TX772.D865 2005
641.8´654 — dc22

                                  2005002245

10 9 8 7 6 5 4 3 2

Published by Lark Books, A Division of
Sterling Publishing Co., Inc.
387 Park Avenue South, New York, N.Y. 10016

Text © 2005, Rose Dunnington
Photography © 2005, Lark Books

Distributed in Canada by Sterling Publishing,
c/o Canadian Manda Group, 165 Dufferin Street
Toronto, Ontario, Canada M6K 3H6

Distributed in the United Kingdom by GMC Distribution Services,
Castle Place, 166 High Street, Lewes, East Sussex, England BN7 1XU

Distributed in Australia by Capricorn Link (Australia) Pty Ltd.,
P.O. Box 704, Windsor, NSW 2756 Australia

If you have questions or comments about this book, please contact:
Lark Books
67 Broadway
Asheville, NC 28801
(828) 253-0467

Manufactured in China

ISBN 13: 978-1-57990-627-6
ISBN 10: 1-57990-627-3

For information about custom editions, special sales, premium and corporate purchases, please contact Sterling Special Sales
Department at 800-805-5489 or specialsales@sterlingpub.com.

Dedication

I'd like to dedicate this book to Katherine Fairfax Wright, in honor of our friendship, which started with all those afternoons of baking cookies when we got off the school bus.

Contents

Introduction 8

Getting Started
Set-up 10
Safety 11
Cookie Equipment 12
Reading a Recipe 14
Measuring 16
Mixing 18
Working with Dough 20
Baking 24
Decorating 26

Wild & Crazy Cookies!
Sugar Cookies 30
Bugs! 32
Creepy Cookies 34
Planet Earth 36
Marbles 36
Fine Art 37
Day at the Beach 38
Incredible Edible Puzzle 39
Flower Power 40
Stained-Glass Stars 42
Mix & Match Faces 43
How Ya Feelin'? 44
Fall Leaves 45
Out of This World 46
Say It! 47
Peek-A-Boo Jelly Valentines 48
Thumbprints 49
Princess Tea Party 50

Wild Kingdom 52
Eggstravaganza 53
Cityscape 54
Under the Sea 56
Winter Wonderland 58
Snowman 59
Pet Party 60

Chewy, Chunky, Yummy Cookies

The Very Best Chocolate Chip Cookies Ever
TVBCCCE 64
Turtles 65
You Bet Your Butterscotch 65
Candy Bar Chunks 65
Almost Too Good to Be True 65
Every Flavor Jellybeans 65

The Ultimate Chocolate Cookies
Melt in Your Mouth 66
Chocolate Whiteout 67
A Little Nutty 67
Grasshoppers 67
Very Cherry 67

Peanut Butter Pandemonium
Perfectly Peanut-Buttery 68
Kiss Me 69
Freckle Face 69
Extra Nutty 69

Heavenly Cookies
Applesauce Cookies 70
Coconutty Sweetness 71
Gadzooks Granola 71

Yummy Oatmeal-Raisin Cookies
Original Recipe 72
Cinnapple 73

Trail Mix **73**
My Mom's Holiday Cookies **73**
Everything but the Kitchen Sink **73**

So-Good Sandwiches
Ice Cream Craving **74**
PB&J **75**
Ultimate Peppermint Patty **75**
Tropical Paradise **75**

Gingerrific
Goodness Gracious! **76**
Tropical Treat **76**
Lemony **76**
Gingerbread People **77**
Sandcastle **78**

No-Bake Cookies
Chocolate Chip **80**
Pick Your Chips **81**
Toss Your Cookies **81**

Cool, Cool Cookies
Spirals **83**
Stripes **84**
Checkerboard **85**
Bull's-eye **86**
Bodacious Bouquet **87**

Party Down
Cookie Making Party **88**
Pizza **91**
Super Chewy Chunky **91**
Breakfast Cookies **92**
Cookie Gifts **93**

Glossary 94
Acknowledgments 95
Metrics 95
Index 96

Introduction

It's cookie time! Everybody's favorite treats are even better when you make them yourself. And guess what? It's easy.

I should know. I've been baking my whole life. When I was a little girl, my mom made desserts at a fancy restaurant. Then I grew up and went to *culinary* school, and I made desserts at a fancy restaurant. What happened in between? Well, I baked all kinds of things — cakes, pies, breads, and, yes, lots and lots of cookies. And I didn't always bake alone. I have six younger brothers and sisters. (That's right, I said six). We had tons of fun making cookies. You will, too.

This book is easy to use, whether you already know how to bake or are just learning. The Getting Started section has instructions for every detail of making cookies, with lots of pictures to show you what to do. Learn about equipment, reading a recipe, measuring, mixing, baking, and decorating. Discover cool tricks, such as how to freeze cookie dough so you can have fresh-baked cookies anytime.

There are some baking words that you've probably heard before, but you might not know exactly what they mean. I've put these terms in italics, and you can look them up in the glossary.

Once you know the basics, making cookies is easy as pie. (Actually, cookies are easier than pie.) The book is divided into chapters of recipes for making 75 different cookies.

Wild & Crazy Cookies! includes shaped, colored, and decorated cookies that are unlike any you've seen before. Find cookies for any time of the year, from spring flowers to winter snowflakes, plus cookies guaranteed to make any day more fun. Plus, I threw in no-bake recipes that are simple to make, delicious to eat, and totally gross to look at.

Chewy, Chunky, Yummy Cookies is a collection of more than two dozen recipes for everything from peanut butter and chocolate cookies to oatmeal-raisin cookies with apple chunks. The Cool, Cool Cookies chapter has recipes for fancy, funky cookies that look complicated but aren't. They taste great.

Want an excuse to invite friends over and make (and eat!) giant cookies? You'll find ideas and instructions in Party Down. That chapter includes a section on giving cookies as gifts.

But don't think you need a special occasion to make cookies. All you need is some time — less time than you think— ingredients, and your appetite. Make the recipes often, so you can decide which is your favorite. Hmm, is it Candy Bar Chunks, Peek-a-boo Jelly Valentines, or My Mom's Holiday Cookies? Maybe you're crazy for ice cream sandwiches. Or do you go for the classics, like The Very Best Chocolate Chip Cookies Ever?

Get in the kitchen already. What are you waiting for? It's cookie time.

Getting Started

It's easier and more fun to cook in an organized workspace. And, when you cook safely and clean up after yourself, your parents will see that you're responsible enough to use the kitchen. Then they'll let you do it again. Follow the Set-up and Safety tips I use in my kitchen.

Set-up

- Always clean your hands before touching any food, *utensils*, or baking tools. Dry your hands well.

- Wear an apron to protect your clothes.

- Have a place ready for dirty dishes.

- Clean up spills as soon as they happen.

- Learn how to use your oven. (Ask an adult—they like to feel useful.)

- Have a clear counter space with hot pads ready for a hot cookie sheet. There's nothing worse that pulling a perfect batch of cookies out of the oven, then freaking out trying to find a place to put the cookie sheet down before your hands get too hot.

Safety

- Always use two oven mitts to move a cookie sheet in or out of the oven. The door and sides of the oven get just as hot as the racks and the cookie sheet.

- If you burn a finger, stick it in a glass of iced water.

- If you have a problem in the kitchen, ask an adult for help.

Professional Chef Tip

If an oily spill still feels slick after you've wiped it up, sprinkle a little salt on it. The salt will stop you from slipping while you keep working, and you can sweep it up later.

Cookie Equipment

These are the tools you'll use most often to make cookies. You don't need equipment that looks just like what you see on these pages, but you do need tools that get the job done.

Mixing Tools

Mixing the ingredients is the first step in cookie making. There are lots of options for what tools to use.

Bowls hold the ingredients you measure out, and sometimes you'll mix right in the bowls.

This is a **freestanding electric mixer.** You can use a hand-held electric mixer or a fork instead, if that's what you have.

Dough Tools

There are recipes in this book that ask you to play with the dough before you bake it. Here are special tools to use.

A **pastry brush** (or basting brush) lets you brush on Egg Wash to join pieces of dough. (You'll read about that in Working with Dough on page 18.)

You'll use a **rolling pin** to roll your blob of dough into a smooth, even sheet that's ready to be cut.

A **rubber spatula** is a good tool for pushing sticky dough down the sides of a mixing bowl. (You'll also use it to spread icing. See Decorating on page 26.)

A **wooden baking board** (or cutting board) is the perfect surface for rolling out dough. You can use a clean countertop instead, but make sure it's absolutely clean and dry.

A **large wooden spoon** is great for mixing chunky ingredients.

Cutting Tools

You'll need these tools when cutting your dough into fun shapes.

Cookie cutters come in every shape and are easy to use.

A **pizza wheel** is a good tool for cutting large or curvy shapes.

A **paring knife** is just the right size for making small, precise cuts.

Baking Tools

Your cookies are almost cookies! Use the following equipment for baking awesome cookies.

A **timer** should be set to the lowest baking time indicated in the recipe. You could use your watch, but the cool thing about a timer is that it DINGS so you don't forget to check on your cookies.

A **cookie sheet** (or baking sheet) is required. It's what you put your dough pieces on when you are ready to bake.

Cookie Time Tools

The cookies are ready! Or are they? Have this equipment handy for your final steps.

A **cooling rack** looks like an oven rack, but has stands on the bottom so the rack is raised off whatever you set it on. You move your too-hot-to-touch cookies to this rack so they can cool. If you don't have one, cool your cookies on a brown paper bag.

A **metal spatula** helps you take super-hot cookies off the mega-hot cookie sheet.

Reading a Recipe

A *recipe* is a list of ingredients and instructions for making food. You need to know how to read recipes if you want make awesome cookies.

1) Titles and Yields

Recipes are usually written the same way. First comes the title. Right under the name is the word *yield*, followed by a number. This number tells you how many cookies the recipe will make. Depending on how big you make your cookies, your yield might be different from the one on the recipe.

2) Ingredients

Next on the recipe come the *ingredients*. The ingredients are listed in the order they are used. The recipe will also tell you how much of each ingredient you need. (Read about measuring on page 16.) Before you begin making a recipe, make sure you have the ingredients.

3) Equipment

What you use to mix and cook your food is *equipment*. Bowls, a mixer, and spatulas are all equipment. Each recipe in this book lists the equipment that you need. (I didn't list "oven" because you know you need one of those, right?)

4) Instructions

After the ingredients and equipment, the recipe lists what you do to make the cookies. Read all of the steps before you start. You might find out that the dough has to sit in the refrigerator for a whole day before it gets baked. You want to know that before you get started. The instructions also tell you at what temperature to bake, and for how long.

Substitutions

Is it okay to use margarine instead of butter? What about white sugar instead of brown? Using one ingredient in place of another is called a substitution. *You can make substitutions—just remember that they'll change the way the cookies feel, taste, and look.*

For example, brown sugar makes Melt-in-Your-Mouth cookies on page 66 soft and chewy. If you use white sugar, you'll get crispy cookies. (Maybe that's how you like them!) Instead of vanilla extract, you could use another flavor. (Peppermint?) The only difference will be the taste—but it will be a big difference.

Some substitutions don't work as well. For instance, using cooking oil instead of butter results in flat, crunchy cookies. That's because you've replaced a solid (butter) with a liquid (oil), changing the proportions of the recipe. For guaranteed yummy cookies that are "just right," follow the recipes I've created for you.

The Very Best Chocolate Chip Cookies Ever

Yield: 24

Ingredients

1 stick softened butter
1/3 c granulated sugar
1/3 c light brown sugar
1 egg
1 tsp vanilla extract
1/2 tsp baking soda
1/4 tsp salt
1 1/4 c flour
1 c chocolate chips

Equipment

Measuring cups and spoons
2 greased cookie sheets
Mixing bowls
Mixer or fork
Spoon

1 Preheat the oven to 375° F.

2 Cream the butter and sugar in a large mixing bowl.

3 Add the egg and vanilla to the creamed butter and sugar. Blend the ingredients well.

4 Mix the flour, salt, and baking soda in the other mixing bowl. Add this dry mixture to the wet mixture. Blend it well. You have cookie dough! Now mix the chocolate chips into the dough.

5 Spoon the dough onto the cookie sheets to make these drop cookies. Bake for 8 to 10 minutes.

6 Allow the cookies to cool before eating them.

Measuring

Want delicious cookies? Then use the right amount of each ingredient in your recipe. Luckily, this is easy to do.

What and How Much

Before you can measure an ingredient, you need to know what it is and how much of the ingredient you'll use. Liquids (vanilla extract, water) and solids (flour, sugar) require different measuring tools. Most recipes call liquids *wet ingredients*. Measure them in glass or see-through plastic measuring cups. Solids are called *dry ingredients*. You measure them in scoop-type measuring cups. *Volume* is how much space something takes up. Most cooking measurements are in volume. Cups, tablespoons, and teaspoons measure volume. Let's go over some translations of measuring abbreviations.

c = cup

T = tablespoon

tsp = teaspoon
   3 tsp equal 1 T

oz = ounce or ounces

° = degrees of temperature

F = Fahrenheit, the temperature scale used by most American ovens

Wet Ingredients

The measuring tools you'll use for wet ingredients usually have tons of lines and numbers, with *mL* and *oz* beside the numbers. Figure out which line marks the measurement you need to make, and pour up to that line. The best way to get an accurate measurement is to put the cup on a stable surface and put your eyes even with the top of the liquid.

What About Butter?

Butter is often the first ingredient in a cookie recipe, but you don't have to measure it for these recipes. Why not? The recipes that use butter call for one-half to one whole stick of it, and most butter is sold in sticks. Easy, huh? But you have to remember to soften the butter so it will cream well. (Read about that in Mixing, beginning on page 18.)

container, use a spoon to put the flour in the measuring cup.

Sometimes a recipe calls for things like brown sugar or coconut to be *packed*. This means you should jam the ingredient down in the measuring cup to fit as much in there as you can. It's fun to pack ingredients, but only do it when the recipe calls for it.

Dry Ingredients

To measure a dry ingredient, first make sure there are no lumps in it. (You can crush it with your clean hands or a fork.) Then dip your measuring scoop or cup into the ingredient. Use the flat edge of a table knife against the rim of the cup to push the extra off the top. Most solids like sugar and oatmeal are easy to measure this way.

It may seem like the amounts of *baking soda* and *baking powder* are too tiny to do anything. Don't be fooled! These are the most powerful ingredients. Too much will make your cookies taste terrible. Too little will make the cookies flat and dense.

You can pour chocolate chips and nuts into a measuring cup, but you shouldn't pour flour. It will make a mess. If your measuring cup won't fit in the flour

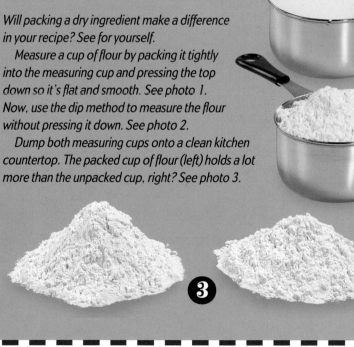

Test It

Will packing a dry ingredient make a difference in your recipe? See for yourself.

Measure a cup of flour by packing it tightly into the measuring cup and pressing the top down so it's flat and smooth. See photo 1. Now, use the dip method to measure the flour without pressing it down. See photo 2.

Dump both measuring cups onto a clean kitchen countertop. The packed cup of flour (left) holds a lot more than the unpacked cup, right? See photo 3.

Mixing

Got your ingredients? Then it's mixing time. Mix recipe ingredients in the order they're listed. If you mess up it's okay to add ingredients later. The cookies will taste the same, but the texture will be different. Who knows— maybe you'll like them better that way.

Mixing Butter and Sugar

Okay, the instructions say, "Cream the butter and sugar." It makes no sense! There isn't even any cream on the ingredients list! Well, in this case, *cream* is an action, not an ingredient.

In order to cream easily, butter must be *softened*. That means the butter should be room temperature and feel squishy like cream cheese. Leave it out on the counter for a few hours, or microwave it on a plate for 20 seconds. (Just soften the butter— don't make it melt or cook.) By the way, all my recipes use regular butter (salted, not unsalted).

What You Need
Softened butter
Sugar
Mixer or fork
Mixing bowl

1 Put the softened butter in the bowl. (Save the wrapper. You'll use it to grease your cookie sheet.) Add the correct amount of sugar to the bowl. See photo 1.

2 Mix on medium speed until the mixture is creamy. See photo 2. Creaming takes 2 to 4 minutes.

If you use an electric mixer, follow these rules:

Dry your hands before you plug or unplug the mixer.

When you're done with a step, turn the mixer off while the beaters are still in the mixture. This will help you avoid splattering.

Unplug the mixer before you attach or remove the beaters from a handheld mixer, and before you clean the mixer.

Turn the mixer off before you put your fingers or any utensil in the bowl.

Don't put an electric mixer in water. To clean an electric mixer, unplug it and wipe it off with a soapy, wrung-out sponge or towel.

Mixing Wet Ingredients

Now's the time to add the wet ingredients, such as *eggs* or *vanilla extract*.

What You Need
Wet ingredients
Measuring tools
Creamed butter and sugar
   (in a mixing bowl)
Mixer or fork

1 Measure out the correct amount of the wet ingredients and add them to the bowl of creamed butter and sugar. See photo 3.

2 Mix on the lowest speed, and then change to a medium speed. (If you're using a fork, the speed doesn't matter.) The mixture will be chunky, clumpy, gross looking, and then become completely smooth.

Preheat

If you are starting to mix ingredients, it's time to preheat the oven. Make sure the oven rack that you'll put the cookie sheet on is in the middle of the oven. (See Where in the Oven? on page 24 for more information.) Then set your oven to the temperature called for in the recipe.

Mixing Dry Ingredients

Most of the recipes in this book include *flour*. They also include other basic dry ingredients, such as baking soda or baking powder.

What You Need
Dry ingredients
Measuring tools
Mixing bowl
Fork
Mixture of wet ingredients
   (in a mixing bowl)
Mixer or fork

1 Measure the correct amounts of dry ingredients and pour them in the empty mixing bowl. Stir with the fork. See photo 4.

2 Pour the dry mixture into the bowl of wet mixed ingredients (the creamed butter, sugar, egg, etc.). See photo 5.

3 Mix on the lowest speed for a few seconds, and then move up to a medium speed. (If you're mixing with a fork, your speed doesn't matter.)

4 Mix until the color is the same throughout and there are no dry clumps. You've got dough! See photo 6. This could take 1 minute or more.

Mixing Goodies

Some recipes call for goodies, such as chocolate chips, raisins, and nuts. Measure them into your dough and mix on low speed until it looks as if there's an equal amount of goodies throughout.

Working with Dough

Want to DO something with the delicious dough you've made? First you'll need to *grease* the cookie sheet. It sounds gross, but it's fun — and it stops your cookies from sticking. Rub the inside of the butter wrapper on the cookie sheet. If you threw the butter wrapper away, rub on a little vegetable oil, or use an unflavored cooking or baking spray.

Drop Cookies

Drop cookies are put on the cookie sheet a spoonful of dough at a time. (A tablespoon works great.)

Spooning the Dough

It's as easy as it looks.

What You Need
Dough
Spoon
Another spoon (optional)
Greased cookie sheet

1 Scoop up some dough with the spoon. Use your clean finger or another spoon to push the dough onto the cookie sheet. See photo 1. Leave enough room around the cookies to put an imaginary cookie in between the real ones, because the cookies will spread as they bake. You're ready to bake!

2 Want giant cookies? Use an ice-cream scoop to put the dough on the cookie sheet, and then flatten the mound with the palm of you hand. (If you don't flatten them, the centers will not cook.) Leave 2 inches clear around each giant dough mound.

Cutout Cookies

Cutout cookies are exactly what they sound like. Chill the dough, roll it out, and then use *cutting tools* to make any shape you want.

Chilling the Dough

Using cold dough is the trick to making the cleanest cuts. (Clean cuts let you make hippos that look like hippos, instead of unrecognizable blobs.)

What You Need
Flour
Dough
Plastic wrap
Flat surface

1 Dip your hands in the flour. The flour will help stop the dough from sticking to you.

2 Divide the dough into equal halves. Shape each half into a ball.

3 Wrap each ball in plastic wrap. Then mash each ball into a patty about 1 inch thick. See photo 2.

4 Put the two dough patties in the refrigerator for at least 15 minutes. Use the waiting time to clean up and set up your work area for the next step.

Rolling the Dough

Your chilled dough is ready for rolling. So what are you waiting for? This is my favorite part of making cutout cookies.

What You Need
Chilled dough
Flour
Flat surface
Rolling pin

1 Sprinkle flour on the flat surface. The flour keeps the dough from sticking. I pile a little extra flour on the board so I can grab more when I need it. See photo 3.

2 Remove one of the dough patties from the refrigerator. Unwrap it and put it on the flat, floured surface.

3 Rub flour on the rolling pin. Don't be stingy.

4 Starting in the middle of the dough patty and pushing away from its middle, begin rolling out the dough. See photo 4.

5 It doesn't take much muscle or time to roll the dough until it's all approximately 1/4 inch thick. See photo 5.

Cutting the Dough

Use cutting tools (cookie cutters, pizza wheel, or paring knife), or use a pattern and a cutting tool together. To make a pattern, draw or trace the shape you want on cardboard, and then use scissors to cut the shape out.

No matter what you use, any time the dough gets hard to work with, rewrap it in plastic and put it in the refrigerator for 10 minutes.

What You Need
Rolled-out dough
Flour
Flat surface
Cutting tools
Spatula
Greased cookie sheet

1 Most cookie cutters have a sharp side. Find that side. Dip it in flour so it doesn't get gunked up with dough. See photo 6. (Do this with whatever cutting tool you use, repeating as necessary.)

2 If you are using a cookie cutter, press it straight down into the dough. Then lift the cutter straight up and away from the dough. See photo 7. If the cookie stays inside the cutter, you can just carry it to the greased cookie sheet and gently push the cutout cookie out onto the sheet.

3 If you're using a pizza wheel or paring knife, cut by moving the tool away from yourself. See photo 8. If you've made a pattern out of cardboard, lay the pattern on the dough, hold it in place, and cut around it.

4 When you cut out multiple cookies, make your cuts in the dough as close together as possible, so you don't have a lot of leftover dough pieces. See photo 9.

5 Use the spatula or your hands to move the cutout shapes to the greased cookie sheet. Leave about 1 inch on all sides of each cookie. See photo 10.

6 If you don't like the shape you made, try again. Squish it up with the scraps of remaining dough. Chill the dough, roll it out, and cut again.

Constructing One-of-a-Kind Shapes

Put dough shapes together to construct any crazy shape you want. Just use the Cutting the Dough instructions, and then use the Egg Wash recipe and Piecing Together Dough instructions.

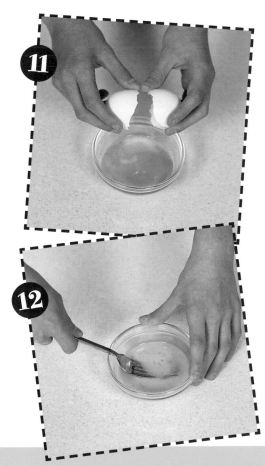

Egg Wash

Egg Wash works like edible glue. (You can also brush Egg Wash lightly on raw dough to make your cookies shiny after they are baked.)

What You Need
Egg
Small bowl
Fork
Water
Measuring spoons

1 Crack the eggshell and drop the egg white and egg yolk into the bowl. See photo 11. Discard the eggshell.

2 Add 1 tablespoon of water to the egg. Beat the mixture with a fork until you've blended the egg white, egg yolk, and water. See photo 12.

Piecing Together Dough

It's easiest to piece dough together on the greased cookie sheet. Then you don't have to worry about moving the finished shape.

What You Need
Egg Wash (in a small bowl)
Cutout cookie dough
Greased cookie sheet
Pastry brush (or fingers)

1 Put the cutout dough pieces on the greased cookie sheet. Press down lightly in the places where the dough will overlap when you join the pieces. Use the pastry brush to paint on a little Egg Wash there. See photo 13. A little goes a long way! Don't slosh or pour it on—paint it on.

2 Press the dough pieces into place in the Egg Wash. See photo 14.

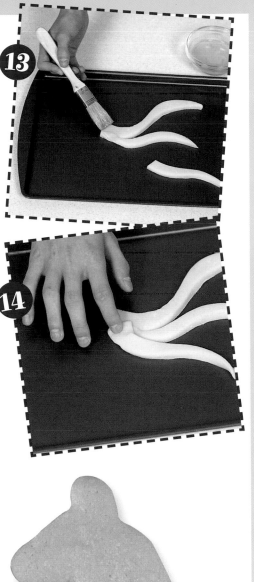

Baking

If your dough is on a greased cookie sheet, it's time for your oven to do its share of the work. You are only minutes away from fresh cookies!

Don't Peek

Don't open the oven door before the timer dings. Each time you open the door you let the heat out from the top of the oven. That means you could burn the bottoms of your cookies while leaving their tops and centers raw. (Of course, if that sounds yummy to you, go for it.)

Is the Oven Ready?

If the oven was set on preheat at the temperature called for in the recipe, turn it to bake. Forgot to preheat? Do it now. Speaking of temperature, most ovens aren't precise when it comes to temperature. If your cookies spread out too much or take longer than expected, set the temperature 5 degrees higher next time. If your cookies burn around the edges after the shortest recommended baking time, set the temperature 5 degrees lower.

Where in the Oven?

Put the cookie sheet on the oven rack in very middle of the oven. See photo above. (If you didn't move the baking rack to the middle rung before preheating, ask an adult to put on oven mitts and move it.) You want the heat from the bottom of the oven to reach the cookies on all sides. You can bake two or more sheets of cookies at the same time. Just put the sheets side-by-side on the baking rack. Don't let them touch (that would block the heat). If there's not enough room in your oven, bake the cookies one sheet at a time.

Timing

Set a timer for the least amount of time called for in the recipe. When the timer dings, check the cookies. You'll know the cookies are done when they're slightly brown on the edges and they don't look wet on top. If they don't look done, leave them in the oven for 2 more minutes.

Knowing when things are done is part of the art of baking. You get better at it with practice. Try taking one *batch* out when it looks a little raw, but after it's baked for the minimum time called for in the recipe. Take the next batch out when it looks really cooked. After they cool, taste both batches and decide which cookies you like the best.

Cooling

When the cookies are done, put on the oven mitts and remove the cookie sheets from the oven. Turn the oven off. Let the cookies set-up for a few minutes on the cookie sheet. Then use a metal spatula to move them to the cooling rack. See photo above right. You can eat the cookies when they are warm, but let them cool completely before decorating. (A hot cookie will melt icing.)

Storing

If you need to store your cookies, wait until they are cool, and then put them in an airtight container. (Resealable plastic bags work well.) Store them at room temperature for up to a week, or up to a month in the freezer. Don't keep cookies in the refrigerator—the cool temperature makes cookies get stale fast.

Fresh Cookies Anytime

Cookies are the best when they are still warm from the oven. Here's how to be ready to bake and eat fresh cookies anytime:

1 *Make the dough when you have spare time. Place your cutout or drop cookie dough on a greased cookie sheet. (Don't leave space between the cookies. Get as many as you can on each sheet.)*

2 *Put the cookie sheet in the freezer for 2 hours, or until the dough is frozen solid.*

3 *Put the frozen dough in a plastic freezer bag. Store it in the freezer.*

4 *When you want cookies, bake the dough according to the recipe, but add 2 to 4 minutes of baking time.*

Decorating

Make a cookie fancy, funky, funny—anything you like—by decorating it. One of my favorite decorations is icing. It's delicious, and you can make it any color you like.

Buttercream Icing

Here's my recipe.

What You Need
2 sticks softened butter
4 c powdered sugar
2 tsp vanilla
3 T milk
Mixer or fork
Mixing bowl

1 Put all the ingredients in a mixing bowl. See photo 1.

2 Mix until you have a creamy, fluffy concoction. See photo 2.

Cookie Glue

Use this icing to build cookie creations. It's creamy when you make it, but it dries stiff and strong. First you need to learn to *separate eggs*.

Separating Eggs

Once you've done this, you have a major chef skill.

What You Need
Egg
1 small bowl

1 Crack the egg over a small, empty bowl, and open it up, so the two eggshell halves are little cups. Some of the *egg white* (the clear goop) will fall into the bowl.

2 Gently pass the *egg yolk* (the yellow part) from one half of the shell to the other. Let the white ooze out into the bowl. After a few passes, you'll have all the white in the bowl, and the yolk in the shell. (Throw away the yolk and shell.)

Making Cookie Glue

Ready with your egg white? Okay. Proceed.

What You Need
1 ¼ c confectioners' sugar
1 egg white
Mixing bowl
Mixer or whisk

1 Put the sugar and egg white in the bowl. If you're using a stand-up mixer, use the *whisk attachment*.

2 Combine the ingredients with the mixer on the lowest speed, and then whip the mixture on high until it's snow-white and fluffy. See photo 3. This takes 4 to 5 minutes, or longer if you use a *whisk*.

3 Air dries this icing out fast, making it crusty, so store Cookie Glue in an airtight container. It will keep for up to one day.

Coloring Icing

A drop or more of food coloring and a spoon is all it takes to change the color of icing. For very bright colors, use *cake-decorating pastes*. (Sold at cake decorating shops.)

Making and Using a Pastry Bag

I make one bag for each color of icing I need.

What You Need

Waxed paper or
  parchment paper
Flat surface
Scissors
Icing

1 Lay one sheet of paper flat. Fold up one bottom corner to create a triangle. Cut along the fold. See photo 4.

2 Bring one point from the base (long side) of the triangle toward the other point of the triangle's base. See photo 5.

Piping Primer

Drawing on a cookie with icing is called *piping*. Piping is really fun, and with practice you'll get the hang of it fast. Most chefs make their own pastry bag from a piece of waxed paper. If you own or want to buy a pastry bag (one that you won't throw away after each use), you will also need tips to attach to the bag. Follow the instructions that come with the pastry bag. If you want a smooth layer of icing, spread it on with a butter knife or rubber spatula.

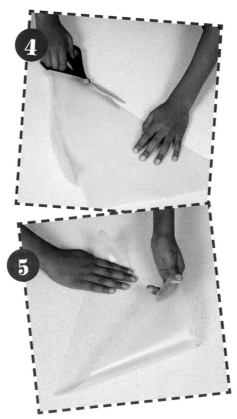

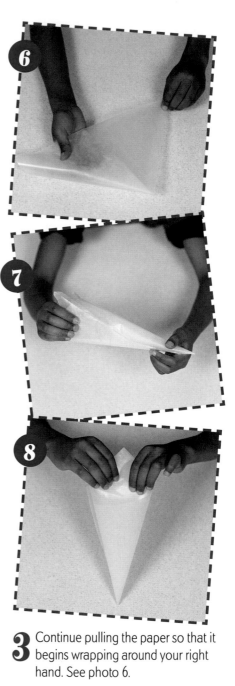

3 Continue pulling the paper so that it begins wrapping around your right hand. See photo 6.

4 Shuffle the paper so that the inside piece is tightening while the outer piece continues to wrap into a cone. See photo 7.

5 Fold in the pieces at the top of the cone to hold the shape in place. See photo 8.

6 Use a spatula or spoon to fill the bag half full with icing. See photo 6. Push the icing down into the tip to avoid air pockets.

7 Fold up the end of the bag to seal it. Cut the tip to make a small hole. See photo 10.

8 Practice piping on a sheet of waxed paper. See photo 11. You'll hold the pointy end of the pastry bag with one hand to guide it and use your other hand to squeeze the end of the bag. Continue folding the bag as it empties.

9 When you are finished practicing, use the same technique on a cookie. See photo 12. Throw the pastry bag away after you use and/or eat all the icing out of it.

Coloring Dough

Make a cookie any color. Just mix food coloring into the dough while it's in the mixing bowl. Food coloring can stain your fingers, so wash your hands as soon as possible.

Wild & Crazy Cookies!

Sure, perfectly round, plain cookies taste great. But why do they need to look boring? Why not make cookies look as good as they taste? This chapter is the solution to dull cookies. It has recipes for 40 of the coolest-looking cookies ever made. (Take a peek at pages 32 to 60.)

Use the basic sugar cookie recipe and instructions here to make the dough for these cookies.

Some of the cookies have extra ingredients for making the decorations. How will you know what to use and what to do? Just look on the recipe for each cookie. If you are unsure about any of the steps, turn back to Getting Started (pages 10 to 29) for a reminder.

Sugar Cookies

Yield: 24 cookies

Ingredients
1 stick softened butter
¾ c sugar
1 egg
2 tsp vanilla
1 ½ c flour
¼ tsp salt

Equipment
Measuring cups and spoons
2 greased cookie sheets
Large mixing bowl
Small mixing bowl
Mixer or fork
Flat surface
Plastic wrap
Flour
Rolling pin
Cutting tools

1 Preheat the oven to 375° F.

2 Cream the softened butter and sugar in a large mixing bowl. (See page 18.)

3 Add the egg and vanilla to the creamed butter and sugar. Blend the ingredients well.

4 Mix the dry ingredients in the other mixing bowl. Add this dry mixture to the wet mixture. Blend it well. You have dough!

5 Chill the dough for 15 minutes, and then roll and cut the dough as called for in your recipe. Place the dough on the greased cookie sheets.

6 Bake for 8 to 10 minutes.

7 Allow the baked cookies to cool before decorating or eating them.

Bugs!

Yield: 3 or more of each insect

Ingredients
1 batch Sugar Cookie dough
  (page 31)
Egg Wash (page 23)
1 batch Buttercream Icing
  (page 26)
Food coloring
Chocolate jimmies

Equipment
Several small bowls
Flat surface
Plastic wrap
Flour
Rolling pin
Bug-shaped or round cookie cutters
Pastry brush (or fingers)
2 greased cookie sheets
Pastry bags (page 28)

1 Preheat the oven to 375° F. Divide the dough and color each section of dough (see page 29) to match the insects you're making. I made six different colors.

2 Wrap and chill the dough.

3 Roll out the dough. You can use bug-shaped cookie cutters, or you can make your own bugs. Try both! Build the cookies on the greased cookie sheets. Make a snail by rolling a snake of dough. See photo 1. Roll a second, longer snake and curl like a snail's shell. Make a caterpillar by gluing little rounds of dough together with Egg Wash. See photo 2. Glue the snail and caterpillar joints together by brushing on Egg Wash. Make a butterfly by gluing pairs of round wings to a body with Egg Wash.

4 Brush the cookies with the Egg Wash before you bake them so they will be shiny. Bake for 8 to 10 minutes.

5 Allow the baked cookies to cool before decorating or eating them. I used icing to draw eyes and designs on the bugs. To make antennae instead of eyes, pipe pairs of dots on the butterfly heads and stick a jimmy in each dot. See photo 3.

Creepy Cookies

Yield: 2 or more of each

Ingredients

1 batch Sugar Cookie dough (page 31)
1 batch Buttercream Icing (page 26)
Food coloring
Handful small red candies
Handful pretzel sticks

Equipment

Flat surface
Plastic wrap
Flour
Rolling pin
Four sizes of round cookie cutters
2 greased cookie sheets
Small bowls
Pastry bags (page 28)

1 Preheat the oven to 375° F. Wrap and chill the dough for these cutout cookies.

2 Roll out the dough. Cut out four sizes of circles: large for pumpkins, medium for spider bodies and eyeball whites, small for spider heads and irises, and tiny for pupils.

3 Little cookies cook fast, so they need their own cookie sheet. Move the dough pieces onto the greased cookie sheets. Bake the small and tiny pieces for 5 to 7 minutes. Bake the large and medium pieces for 8 to 10 minutes.

4 While the cookies are baking, make icing in these colors: black (a lot), orange (a lot), white (medium amount), blue (small amount), and red (small amount). Look at the finished cookie photos on these pages to see how I used each color.

5 Allow the cookies to cool before decorating them. To make the big round cookies look pumpkin-shaped, spread orange icing on them. Then draw the classic pumpkin shape in black icing on top of the orange icing. See photo 1.

6 Spread black icing on the spiders. Then attach the pretzel "legs." See photo 2. The spider's red-hot mouth is hungry for blood! Use the large cookies for the creepy eyes.

Planet Earth

Yield: 24

Ingredients
1 batch Sugar Cookie dough
  (page 31)
Green and blue food coloring
½ batch Buttercream Icing
  (page 26, optional)
Red food coloring (optional)

Equipment
Medium size bowl
Spoon
Flat surface
Plastic wrap
Flour
Rolling pin
Round cookie cutter
2 greased cookie sheets
Pastry bag (page 28, optional)

1 Preheat the oven to 375°F. Divide the dough in three parts.

2 Use two or three drops of green food coloring to make part of the dough light green. Use four or five drops of blue food coloring to make another part dark blue. Leave the final section of dough white.

3 Wrap and chill the dough.

4 Squish the doughs together a little bit. See photo 1. Don't mix the colors — you don't want to make a new color. Roll out the dough. It will have blue and green swirls, which is what the Earth looks like from outer space. Cut out round Earths and put them on the greased cookie sheets.

5 Bake for 8 to 10 minutes.

6 Allow the cookies to cool before decorating or eating them. I drew a little red icing heart on each cookie to say "I love the Earth."

Marbles

Like this look? You can also make colorful cookies from dough scraps. Separate the scraps into sections; make each section a different color. Then follow steps 4 and 5.

Fine Art

Yield: 6 or more masterpieces

Ingredients
1 batch Sugar Cookie dough
(page 31)
1 batch Buttercream Icing
(page 26)
Food coloring
1 bag black licorice

Equipment
Flat surface
Plastic wrap
Flour
Rolling pin
Pizza wheel or paring knife
Ruler (optional)
2 greased cookie sheets
Butter knife
Small bowls
Small art paintbrush
Scissors

1 Preheat the oven to 375° F. Wrap and chill the dough for these cutout cookies.

2 Roll out the dough. Cut it into rectangles about 3 inches wide by 5 inches long.

3 Put the dough on the greased cookie sheets. Bake for 8 to 10 minutes.

4 Let the cookies cool before decorating them. Use the butter knife or spatula to spread icing on each cookie. Pour a little food coloring into each small bowl. Use a brand new paintbrush to paint masterpieces onto the icing atop each cookie. See photo 1.

5 Cut black licorice with scissors, and put it around the edges of the cookies for a frame. If they look great, take a picture before you gobble them up.

Day at the Beach

Yield: 2 or more of each object

Ingredients
1 batch Sugar Cookie dough
   (page 31)
Egg Wash (page 23)
1 batch Buttercream Icing
   (page 26)
Food coloring

Equipment
Flat surface
Plastic wrap
Flour
Rolling pin
Round cookie cutters
Pastry brush (or fingers)
2 greased cookie sheets
Small bowls
Pastry bags (page 28)

1 Preheat the oven to 375° F. Wrap and chill the dough for these cutout cookies.

2 Roll out the dough. Cut out each cookie shape. To make the umbrella, first cut out a big round cookie. See photo 1. Cut it in half, and then use a little round cutter used to scallop the edges. See photo 2.

3 Attach a dough-snake pole to the umbrella with Egg Wash. The sunglasses are two round cookies connected by a dough nose-piece, attached with Egg Wash. A round cutter makes a beach ball.

4 Move the dough pieces onto the greased cookie sheet. Bake for 8 to 10 minutes.

5 While your cookies are baking, color the icing bright, summery colors. Look at my finished cookies for inspiration. Divide the icing into as many small bowls as you need to make all the colors you want. Blend each color well.

6 Allow the cookies to cool before decorating them.

Incredible Edible Puzzle

Yield: 2 puzzles

Ingredients
1 batch Sugar Cookie dough
(page 31)
1 batch Buttercream Icing
(page 26)
Food coloring

Equipment
Flat surface
Plastic wrap
Flour
Rolling pin
Paring knife or pizza wheel
2 greased cookie sheets
Butter knife

1 Preheat the oven to 375° F. Wrap and chill the dough for these cutout cookies.

2 Roll out your cookie dough. Cut out a very large square. Cut the square into puzzle pieces; they need to fit together, but they should have curvy lines and interesting shapes for each puzzle piece. See photo 1. Cut as many pieces as you like.

3 Move the dough pieces onto the greased cookie sheets. Leave room between the pieces. (The dough will expand as it bakes.)

4 Bake the dough for 8 to 10 minutes.

5 Allow the cookies to cool before decorating them.

6 Pick one color for each puzzle piece, and then make icing in those colors. Spread one icing color in each piece. See photo 2. Let the icing harden for a few minutes. Then mix the pieces up and let your friends put together the edible puzzle.

Flower Power

Yield: 12 or more blooms

Ingredients
1 batch Sugar Cookie dough
  (page 31)
Food coloring
Egg Wash (page 23)

Equipment
Several small bowls
Flat surface
Plastic wrap
Flour
Rolling pin
Flower-shaped or round
  cookie cutters
2 greased cookie sheets
Pastry brush (or fingers)

1 Preheat the oven to 375° F. Separate your cookie dough into a few different batches. Use food coloring to color each batch a different color: make yellow for the flower centers and pick other colors (red, pink, orange, purple, etc.) for the flower petals.

2 Wrap and chill the dough for these cutout cookies.

3 Roll out your colored cookie doughs (one at a time). Cut out petals with round cookie cutters. You can make pointy petals by overlapping round cuts.

4 Construct each cookie on a greased cookie sheets. Press into the dough where you want to connect two pieces of dough. See photo 1. Use Egg Wash like glue to connect the pieces. Put a little yellow ball of dough in the middle of each flower. See photo 2. Brush the whole cookie with the Egg Wash before you bake it. See photo 3. This makes the finished cookie shine.

5 Bake for 8 to 10 minutes.

6 Allow the cookies to cool before eating them.

Stained-Glass Stars

Yield: 32

Ingredients
1 batch Sugar Cookie dough (page 31)
1 bag hard candies
Butter, oil, or unflavored cooking spray

Equipment
Aluminum foil
2 cookie sheets
Flat surface
Plastic wrap
Flour
Rolling pin
Large star cookie cutter
Small star cookie cutter

1 Preheat oven to 375° F. Wrap and chill the dough for these cutout cookies.

2 Grease pieces of aluminum foil the size of your cookie sheets. Crumple them up, and then spread them out flat on the cookie sheets, grease-side up. (The more crumples you have in the foil, the better your stained-glass stars will look.)

3 Roll out the dough. Cut out big stars. Carefully place the cookies on the aluminum foil. Cut small stars out of the middle of the big stars to make big star outlines. See photo 1.

4 Place a hard candy in the middle of each cookie. See photo 2. Bake for 8 to 10 minutes.

5 Let these cookies cool on the cookie sheets instead of a cooling rack. When they're cool, carefully peel them off the aluminum foil.

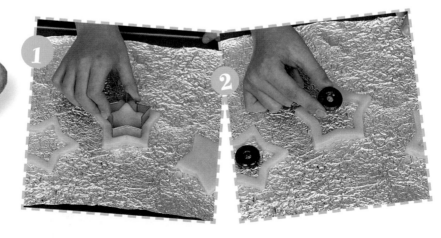

Mix & Match Faces

Yield: 6 or more of each feature

Ingredients
1 batch Sugar Cookie dough (page 31)
1 batch Buttercream Icing (page 26)
Food coloring

Equipment
Flat surface
Plastic wrap
Flour
Rolling pin
Round cookie cutters
2 greased cookie sheets
Small bowls
Butter knife
Pastry bags (page 28)

1 Preheat the oven to 375° F. Wrap and chill the dough for these cutout cookies.

2 Roll out the dough. Make several matching pairs of eyes. Overlap the cuts from round cutters to make eye shapes. See photo 1.

3 Use ropes of dough to make lips. See photo 2. Curl a small piece of dough to make a nose. Make one nose and mouth per pair of eyes and ears.

4 Move the dough pieces onto the greased cookie sheets. Bake for 8 to 10 minutes.

5 Allow the cookies to cool before decorating them.

6 Color the icing with food coloring in a small bowl. For big mouths, I spread on the icing with a butter knife. For eyes, I use pastry bags to pipe on details.

How Ya Feelin'?

Yield: 24

Ingredients
1 batch Sugar Cookie
  dough (page 31)
  ¼ cup chocolate
    chips

Equipment
Flat surface
Plastic wrap
Flour
Rolling pin
Round cutter
Metal spatula
2 greased cookie sheets
Cooling rack
Small bowl
Spoon
Pastry bag (page 28)

1 Preheat the oven to 375° F. Wrap and chill the dough for these cutout cookies.

2 Roll out the dough. Make round cutouts.

3 Move the cutouts onto the greased cookie sheets. Bake for 8 to 10 minutes.

4 Allow the cookies to cool before decorating them.

5 To make the chocolate for the mouths and eyes, pour the chocolate chips into the small bowl. Microwave the chips for 20 seconds. They make not look melted, but they will become a smooth paste when you stir them. See photo 1. The chocolate should be warm and melted, but not burning hot. If it's still lumpy, heat the chips in the microwave for few more seconds.

6 Spoon the chocolate into a pastry bag. Draw faces on the cookies. See photo 2. Have fun creating unexpected expressions.

Fall Leaves

Yield: 24

Ingredients

1 batch Sugar Cookie dough
   (page 31)
Food coloring
¼ cup chocolate chips

Equipment

Five small bowls
Flat surface
Plastic wrap
Flour
Rolling pin
Leaf-shaped or round cookie cutters
2 greased cookie sheets
Spoon
Pastry bag (page 28)

1 Preheat the oven to 375° F. Separate your cookie dough into a few different batches. Use food coloring to color each batch a different fall shade: red, orange, yellow, brown.

2 Wrap and chill the dough for these cutout cookies.

3 Roll out the doughs (one dough at a time). There are lots of leaf-shaped cookie cutters at kitchen stores, especially in the fall. You can make a birch leaf by overlapping cuts from the round cutters.

4 Move the leaf-shaped dough pieces onto the greased cookie sheets. Bake for 8 to 10 minutes.

5 Allow the cookies to cool before decorating them.

6 To make the chocolate for the veins for each leaf, pour the chocolate chips into a small bowl. Microwave the chips for 20 seconds. They make not look melted, but they will become a smooth paste when you stir them. See photo 1 on page 44. The chocolate should be warm and melted, but not burning hot. If it's still lumpy, heat the chips in the microwave for few more seconds.

7 Spoon the chocolate into a pastry bag. Pipe the chocolate lines on the cookies to create the veins for each leaf.

Out of This World

Yield: 1 solar system

Ingredients
1 batch Sugar Cookie dough (page 31)
1 batch Buttercream Icing (page 26)
    Food coloring

Equipment
Flat surface
Plastic wrap
Flour
Rolling pin
Round and star cookie cutters
2 greased cookie sheets
Several small bowls
Butter knife
Large serving plate

1 Preheat the oven to 375° F. Wrap and chill the dough for these cutout cookies.

2 Roll out the dough. Use all different sizes of round cutters, and some small stars. I made a thin snake of dough and attached it to a large cookie to resemble the rings of Saturn.

3 Move the cutout dough pieces onto the greased cookie sheets. Bake for 8 to 10 minutes.

4 Color the icing, using one bowl per color you'll create. I used several different colors, to make each planet unique.

5 Allow the cookies to cool before decorating them. Use the butter knife to spread icing on each cookie.

6 Place the cookies on the plate. Arrange them in the correct order: Mercury, Venus, Earth, Mars, Jupiter, Saturn, Uranus, Neptune, Pluto. (I learned this sentence to memorize the planets: My Very Energetic Mother Just Set Up Nine Pins.)

Say It!

Yield: 4 or more of each symbol

Ingredients
1 batch Sugar Cookie dough (page 31)
Egg Wash (page 23)
1 batch Buttercream Icing (page 26)

Equipment
Flat surface
Plastic wrap
Flour
Rolling pin
Round, arrow-shaped, and star-shaped cookie cutters
Paring knife
Pastry brush (or fingers)
2 greased cookie sheets
Small bowls
Food coloring
Butter knife
Pastry bags (page 28)

1 Preheat the oven to 375° F. Wrap and chill the dough for these cutout cookies.

2 Roll out the dough. Use round cutters to make the Yin-Yang, Have a Nice Day, and Peace Sign cookie shapes. To make the "Reduce, Reuse, Recycle" symbol, cut out three arrows with an arrow-shaped cookie cutter. Put them on a greased cookie sheet and bend them into a circle. Use Egg Wash to glue the dough pieces together. For the shooting star, cut the rainbow shape with a knife, and the star with a cookie cutter. Construct the shooting star shape on the greased cookie sheets, using Egg Wash to glue the dough pieces together.

3 Bake for 8 to 10 minutes.

4 While your cookies are baking, make a batch of icing. Decide how many different colors you want. Separate the icing into enough bowls to make those colors.

5 Allow the cookies to cool before decorating them. Use a butter knife to spread on base colors, such as the green on the recycling symbol and the yellow on the smiley face. Use pastry bags for detailed piping, such as making the rainbow stripes.

Peek-A-Boo Jelly Valentines

Yield: 18

Ingredients
1 batch Sugar Cookie dough
(page 31)
Red jelly (raspberry or strawberry)

Equipment
Flat surface
Plastic wrap
Flour
Rolling pin
Large heart cookie cutter
Small heart cookie cutter
2 greased cookie sheets
Spoon

1 Preheat the oven to 375° F. Wrap and chill the dough for these cutout cookies.

2 Roll out the dough. Cut out an even number of big hearts. Take half of the cutout hearts, and use the small cutters to cut little hearts from them. You now have one big heart and one heart outline per cookie. (You can roll the little hearts back into the dough.)

3 The outlines will cook faster than the solid hearts, so put the outlines and solid hearts on separate cookie sheets. Bake for 8 to 10 minutes.

4 Allow the cookies to cool before decorating them. Spread red jelly on the each big heart. See photo 1. Top the big heart with its outlined heart. See photo 2.

Thumbprints

Yield: 24

Ingredients
1 batch Sugar Cookie dough
  (page 31)
Your favorite jelly or jam

Equipment
Plastic wrap
Spoon
2 greased cookie sheets

1 Preheat the oven to 375° F. Wrap and chill the dough.

2 Take a spoonful of cookie dough and roll it between your hands to make a ball. Put the ball on a greased cookie sheet. Use your thumb to mash a hole in the middle, but not all the way to the bottom. See photo 1.

3 Fill the hole with jelly. See photo 2. Do the same with the rest of the dough. You can use different kinds of jelly to vary the color and flavor of the cookies..

4 Bake for 8 to 10 minutes.

5 Allow the cookies to cool before eating them.

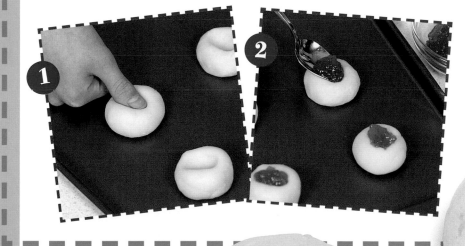

Princess Tea Party

Yield: 18

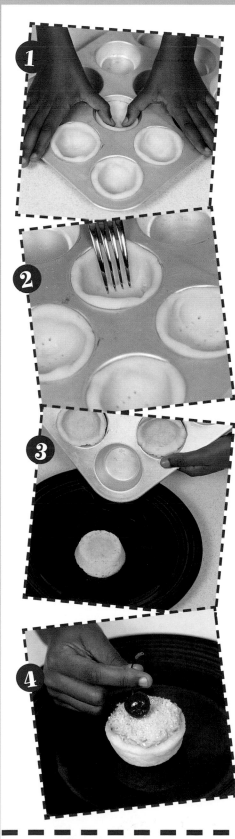

Ingredients
1 batch Sugar Cookie dough
   (page 31)
1 package softened cream cheese (8 oz)
⅓ c jelly or jam
   (your favorite kind)
Sparkle sugar
   (glittery sugar sold in the decorating
   section of a grocery store)
Cherries (canned or fresh)

Equipment
Plastic wrap
Spoon
2 greased muffin pans
Fork
Mixer or fork
Medium size bowl
Spoon

1 Preheat the oven to 375° F. Wrap and chill the dough.

2 Put a spoonful of cookie dough into one cup of a muffin pan.

3 Use your thumbs to press the dough against the bottom and sides of the tin to make a little dough cup. Repeat for the rest of the dough. See photo 1.

4 Put the muffin pans in the freezer for five minutes to chill the dough.

5 Take the muffin pans out of the freezer and prick the bottom of each dough cup with a fork. See photo 2. This will help them keep their shape.

6 Bake for 10 to 12 minutes.

7 While the cookies are baking, make the filling. Mix together the cream cheese and jelly on the lowest mixer speed until it's fluffy and all the same color.

8 Let the cookies cool in the muffin pan, and then take them out of the muffin tin by turning the muffin tin at a slight angle. See photo 3. Be careful — they're delicate.

9 Fill the cookies with the cream cheese filling. Top them with sparkle sugar and a cherry. See photo 4.

Wild Kingdom

Yield: 1 or more of each critter

Ingredients
1 batch Sugar Cookie
  dough (page 31)
½ batch Buttercream Icing (page 26)
Food coloring

Equipment
Flat surface
Plastic wrap
Flour
Rolling pin
Animal-shaped cookie cutters
2 greased cookie cookie sheets
Small bowls
Pastry bags (page 28)

1 Preheat the oven to 375° F. Wrap and chill the dough for these cutout cookies.

2 Roll out your dough. Use the cookie cutters to cut out the kinds of animals you want to make.

3 Move the animals onto the greased cookie sheets. Bake for 8 to 10 minutes.

4 Remove the cookie sheets from the oven. Turn the oven off. Let the cookies set for a few minutes, and then move them to the cooling rack. Allow the cookies to cool before decorating them.

5 Make and color the icing in the small bowls. Put icing in the pastry bags and pipe an outline on each animal. Now is the time to "fix" your animal's shape. Look closely at my alligator and my moose. They got a little out of shape while baking, but their icing outlines make them look perfect.

Eggstravaganza

Yield: a dozen eggs

Ingredients
1 batch Sugar Cookie dough (page 31)
1 batch Buttercream Icing (page 26)
Food coloring
1 bag small jellybeans

Equipment
Flat surface
Plastic wrap
Flour
Rolling pin
Large oval cookie cutters, or paring knife and pattern (page 22)
2 greased cookie sheets
Small bowls
Butter knife or spatula
Spoon
Pastry bags (page 28)

1 Preheat the oven to 375° F. Wrap and chill the dough for these cutout cookies.

2 Roll out the dough. Cut out the cookies using the oval-shaped cutter, use the knife to cut freehand, or use a pattern. (I used a pattern.)

3 Move the dough pieces onto the greased cookie sheets. Bake them for 8 to 10 minutes.

4 While your cookies are baking, decide how many different colors you want. Separate the icing into enough bowls to make those colors. Make the colors light pastels by adding just one drop of food coloring to each bowl. Blend well.

5 Allow the cookies to cool before decorating them.

6 Use the butter knife to spread icing on one cookie. Then pick another color of icing and spoon it into the pastry bag. Pipe icing on in the design of stripes, zig-zags, or polka dots. Do the same for the other cookies, choosing colors that look good together. I stuck little jellybeans in the icing to make cool-looking designs.

Cityscape

Yield: 1 skyline

Ingredients
1 batch Sugar Cookie dough (page 31)
1 batch Cookie Glue (page 27)
1 batch Buttercream Icing (page 26)
Food coloring

Equipment
Flat surface
Plastic wrap
Flour
Rolling pin
Pizza cutter
Flower-shaped cookie cutter (optional)
2 greased cookie sheets
Grater
Butter knife
Spice jars or aluminum foil
Small bowls
Rubber spatula or butter knife
Pastry bags (page 28)

1 Preheat oven to 375°F. Wrap and chill the dough for these cutout cookies.

2 Roll out the dough. Cut out different sizes of rectangles. Cut out one triangle to go with each rectangle, making sure the triangle is about one-sixth the size of the rectangle. See photo 1. Each triangle will prop up each finished rectangle cookie like a picture frame. Cut the bushes freehand or use a flower-shaped cutter. (Cut out a flower, and cut the flower in half to make two bushes.) Make a triangle to go with each bush. Make a few extra triangles in case some break after you bake them.

3 Move the dough pieces onto the greased cookie sheets. Bake for 8 to 10 minutes.

4 Allow the cookies to cool before handling them. Check to make sure the triangles have smooth, flat, even edges where they will connect with the back of the rectangle and whatever they stand on. See photo 2.

5 Trim the edges of the triangles as needed with the grater. See photo 3.

6 Glue the triangles to the backs of the rectangles and bushes with glops of Cookie Glue. Prop the triangles up until the glue dries. Lean them against spice jars or balled up aluminum foil. See photo 4. Let the Cookie Glue dry for at least 2 hours.

7 Decide what colors of icing you want to use. Mix up batches of colored icing in the small bowls. (Don't forget green for the bushes.) Holding a cookie carefully in one hand, decorate it's face to look like a building. I used a spatula to spread on a thin layer of icing, and then used a pastry bag to pipe on windows. Do the same for all the buildings. Decorate the bushes to look like, well, bushes.

Under the Sea

Yield: 1 or more of each sea dweller

Ingredients
1 batch Sugar Cookie dough (page 31)
Egg Wash (page 23)
1 batch Buttercream Icing (page 26)
Food coloring
1 bag small gumdrops

Equipment
Flat surface
Plastic wrap
Flour
Rolling pin
Pizza cutter
Paring knife
Round cookie cutters
Pastry brush (or fingers)
2 greased cookie sheets
Small bowls
Butter knife
Pastry bags (page 28)

1 Preheat the oven to 375° F. Wrap and chill the dough for these cutout cookies.

2 Roll out the dough. Cut wavy shapes with a pizza cutter for seaweed and coral. Overlap cuts from a round cutter to make the oval shaped fish body. Attach fins and a tail with Egg Wash. The octopus is made from a round cutter (head) and a pizza cutter (legs). Cut the lobster free hand with the paring knife.

3 Move the sea animals onto the greased cookie sheets. Use Egg Wash to glue the pieces together. Bake for 8 to 10 minutes.

4 While your cookies are baking, decide what colors of icing you want to use. Mix up your batches of colored icing in the small bowls.

5 Allow the cookies to cool before decorating them.

6 Spread the base layer of icing on each cookie. Use a pastry bag for delicate decorating, such as piping the lines on the lobster and fish. I used gumdrops to create raised spines on the wavy coral shapes, and for the whites of the octopus' eyes. I piped black icing on top of the eyes to create the iris (the dark center of the eyes).

Winter Wonderland

Yield: 12 or more snowflakes

Ingredients
1 batch Sugar Cookie
  dough (page 31)
2 c powdered
  sugar
¼ c milk
Sparkle sugar (glittery
  sugar sold with
  decorating
  supplies)

Equipment
Measuring cups
Flat surface
Plastic wrap
Flour
Rolling pin
Snowflake cookie cutters
Wooden skewer
2 greased cookie sheets
Small bowl
Fork
Spoon
1 yard ribbon

1 Preheat the oven to 375° F. Wrap and chill the dough for these cutout cookies.

2 Roll out the dough. Cut the dough with the snowflake cutters. Move the cutouts to the greased cookie sheets.

3 Use the wooden skewer to poke holes in each cookie. See photo 1. Remember that the dough spreads as it bakes, so make the holes big enough so that they won't close as the dough spreads.

4 Bake for 8 to 10 minutes.

5 Mix the powdered sugar and milk together to make a glaze. See photo 2.

6 Spoon a thin layer of glaze on top of each warm cookie. While the glaze is still wet, sprinkle the sparkle sugar all over each cookie. See photo 3. Let the glaze harden.

Snowman

Yield: 6 or more cookies

Ingredients
1 batch Sugar Cookie
   dough (page 31)
Egg Wash (page 23)
1 batch Buttercream Icing
   (page 26)
Small candies
Fruit leather
Dried fruit pieces

Equipment
Flat surface
Plastic wrap
Flour
Rolling pin
Three sizes of round
   cookie cutters
Pastry brush (or fingers)
2 greased cookie sheets
Butter knife

1 Preheat the oven to 375° F. Wrap and chill the dough for these cutout cookies.

2 Roll out the dough. Cut out an even number of big, medium, and small round shapes. Assemble them in the form of snowmen on the cookie sheets. Use Egg Wash to glue the circles together.

3 Bake for 8 to 10 minutes.

4 Allow the cookies to cool before decorating them.

5 Spread a thin layer of icing on your snowmen cookies. Give them eyes, mouths, buttons, and other decorations with the candy and dried fruit pieces. My sister Lilly cut a carrot nose out of fruit leather. Fruit leather also makes good scarves.

Pet Party

Yield: 6 or more of each best friend

Ingredients
1 batch Sugar Cookie
   dough (page 31)
1 batch Buttercream Icing
   (page 26)
1 bag shredded coconut
Food coloring
Candy sprinkles

Equipment
Flat surface
Plastic wrap
Flour
Rolling pin
Dog-shaped and cat-
   shaped cookie cutters
2 greased cookie sheets
Small bowls
Butter knife

1 Preheat the oven to 375° F. Wrap and chill the dough for these cutout cookies.

2 Roll out the dough. Cut out the cookies.

3 Move the dough pieces onto the greased cookie sheets. Bake them for 8 to 10 minutes.

4 While your cookies are baking, decide what color icing you want. Use the food coloring to make your icing that color.

5 Allow the cookies to cool before decorating. Spread a thin layer of icing on the cookies.

6 Next you'll make and add fur. Decide what color fur you want. Put a handful of the coconut in a small bowl and add several drops of food coloring to the coconut. To make orange, I used yellow and red food coloring. See photo 1. Blend the coconut and food coloring with your fingers until the color is the same throughout. See photo 2.

7 Attach the "fur" coconut to the cookies by gently pushing it into the base layer of icing. See photo 3.

8 It's easy to make ears with the candy sprinkles. See photo 4. You can also use sprinkles to add eyes, whiskers, and claws.

Four-footed Friends Treats

Yield: 18 dog bones

Ingredients
3 eggs
½ c milk
¼ c cooking oil
¼ c molasses
2⅔ c whole-wheat flour

Equipment
Large mixing bowl
Mixer or wooden spoon
Flat surface
Rolling pin
Bone-shaped cookie cutters
2 greased cookie sheets

1 Preheat the oven to 350° F. Mix all the wet ingredients together.

2 Add the flour to the wet mixture. Mix well on low speed. This dough is stiff and making it is a real workout if you mix by hand.

3 Roll out the dough. Cut out bone shapes. Move the dough to the greased cookie sheets.

4 Bake for 30 minutes.

5 Allow the cookies to cool completely before giving one to your pets. (Overeating a new treat can upset your pet's stomach. Don't feed your pet more than two cookies each day.) For extra-crunchy cookies, turn off the oven but leave the cookies in there for another 30 minutes.

Chunky, Chewy, Yummy Cookies

Want to makes cookies that are full of goodies — from chocolate chips, candy bar chunks, and butterscotch, to ginger, nuts, and pineapple? Then you've found your favorite part of this book. This chapter has recipes for the chunkiest, chewiest, yummiest cookies you'll ever sink your teeth into.

Each section is based on a type of cookie, such as peanut butter cookies or gingerbread cookies. There are eight basic cookie recipes and 36 variations — including the grossest, ugliest cookies you'll ever make, cookies without added sugar, and a sandcastle cookie.

Usually you use one dough recipe for all the cookies in a section, and simply add extra chunky or chewy ingredients before you bake it. A few times you'll make different dough using the equipment and instructions from the first recipe. How will you know what to use and what to do? Each recipe tells you. If you are unsure about any of the steps, turn back to Getting Started (pages 10 to 29) for a reminder.

The Very Best Chocolate Chip Cookies Ever

That's what you'll find in this section.
They're all based on one recipe.

TVBCCCE

Yield: 24

Ingredients
1 stick softened butter
$1/3$ c granulated sugar
$1/3$ c packed light brown sugar
1 egg
1 tsp vanilla extract
$1/2$ tsp baking soda
$1/4$ tsp salt
1 $1/4$ c flour
1 c chocolate chips

Equipment
Measuring cups
  and spoons
2 greased cookie
  sheets
Mixing bowls
Mixer or fork
Wooden mixing spoon
Spoon

1 Preheat the oven to 375° F.

2 Cream the butter and sugar in a large mixing bowl. (See page 19.)

3 Add the egg and vanilla to the creamed butter and sugar.
Blend the ingredients well.

4 Mix the flour, salt, and baking soda in the other mixing bowl.
Add this dry mixture to the wet mixture. Blend it well. You have cookie dough!
Now mix the chocolate chips into the dough.

5 Spoon the dough onto the greased cookie sheets to make these drop
cookies. Bake for 8 to 10 minutes.

6 Allow the cookies to cool before eating them.

Can something that's already The Very Best get better?
Make the recipes below and taste for yourself.

Turtles
Yield: 24

Ingredients
1 batch TVBCCCE dough minus the
   chocolate chips
⅓ c chocolate chips
⅓ c caramels
⅓ c pecan pieces
Vegetable oil

Equipment
Scissors or paring knife

The combination of chocolate, caramel, and pecans is called "turtle" flavor. Who knows why? (Not me.) Use scissors to cut caramels into chocolate-chip-size pieces. A little vegetable oil on your scissors will stop the candy from sticking to them.

You Bet Your Butterscotch
Yield: 24

Ingredients
1 batch TVBCCCE dough minus the
   choclate chips
1 c butterscotch chips

Don't like chocolate? Okay, when you make TVBCCCE dough, substitute butterscotch chips for all of the chocolate.

Candy Bar Chunks
Yield: 24

Ingredients
1 batch TVBCCCE dough minus the
   chocolate chips
2 candy bars of your choice
Vegetable oil

Equipment
An adult
Paring knife (let the adult handle it)

One regular size candy bar will make about one cup of chunks, but you might want to get two just in case. Drip oil on the knife to stop the candy bar from sticking to it. Cut the candy bar into chunks the size of your littlest toe. It's not easy to cut a candy bar, so get an adult to handle the knife if you need help.

Almost Too Good to Be True
Yield: 24

Ingredients
1 batch TVBCCCE dough minus the
   chocolate chips
½ c unsalted peanuts
½ c bite-size chocolate
   candies of your choice

Mix the peanuts and candies into the dough before spooning the cookies onto the cookie sheets. These cookies are a mouthful.

Every Flavor Jellybeans
Yield: 24

Ingredients
1 batch TVBCCCE dough minus the
chocolate chips
1 c jellybeans

For jellybean lovers.

The Ultimate Chocolate Cookies

Warning: If you don't LOVE chocolate,
don't make these cookies.

Melt in Your Mouth

Yield: 24

Ingredients
1 stick softened butter
¾ c packed light brown sugar
1 egg
1 tsp vanilla extract
¾ c flour
¾ c cocoa powder
½ tsp baking soda
¼ tsp salt

Equipment
Measuring cups and spoons
2 greased cookie sheets
Mixing bowls
Mixer or fork
Spoon

1 Preheat the oven to 375° F.

2 Cream the butter and sugar in a large mixing bowl. (See page 19.)

3 Add the egg and vanilla to the creamed butter and sugar. Blend the ingredients well.

4 Mix the flour, cocoa powder, baking soda, and salt in the other mixing bowl. Add this dry mixture to the wet mixture. Blend it well. You have dough!

5 Spoon the dough for these drop cookies onto the greased cookie sheets. Bake for 8 to 10 minutes.

6 Allow the cookies to cool before eating them.

Make slight but scrumptious changes to the first recipe for more ultimate chocolate flavor.

Chocolate Whiteout
Yield: 24

Ingredients
1 batch Melt in Your Mouth dough
½ c chocolate chips
½ c white chocolate chips

The bright white chocolate chips make these cookies look weird and taste great.

A Little Nutty
Yield: 24

Ingredients
1 batch Melt in Your Mouth dough
¾ c slivered almonds

The nuts add crunch to these ultimate chocolate cookies.

Grasshoppers
Yield: 24

Ingredients
1 stick softened butter
¾ c packed light brown sugar
1 egg
¾ tsp peppermint extract
¾ c flour
¾ c cocoa powder
½ tsp baking soda
¼ tsp salt
¾ c chocolate chips

Using peppermint extract makes for minty fresh cookies. Adding the chocolate chips makes them chewier.

Very Cherry
Yield: 24

Ingredients
1 stick softened butter
¾ c packed light brown sugar
1 egg
⅓ cup cherry preserves, jam, or jelly
1 tsp vanilla extract
¾ c flour
¾ c cocoa powder
½ tsp baking soda
¼ tsp salt

Add the preserves to the dough after you add the egg. These cookies spread out and are very flat after they are baked, so leave extra room between the dough you drop on the cookie sheet.

Peanut Butter Pandemonium

Like the taste of peanut butter? These are the cookies for you.

Perfectly Peanut-Buttery

Yield: 24

Ingredients

1 stick softened butter
½ c granulated sugar
½ c packed light
   brown sugar
1 egg
1 tsp vanilla extract
1 c peanut butter (crunchy or
   smooth)
1 ¼ c flour
½ tsp baking soda
¼ tsp salt

Equipment

Measuring cups and
   spoons
Mixing bowls
Mixer or fork
Fork
2 greased cookie
   sheets
Spoon

1 Preheat the oven to 375° F.

2 Cream the butter and sugar in a large mixing bowl. (See page 19.)

3 Add the egg and vanilla to the creamed butter and sugar. Blend the ingredients well.

4 Add the peanut butter to the wet mixture. Blend well.

5 Mix the dry ingredients in the other mixing bowl. Add this dry mixture to the wet mixture. Blend it well.

6 Roll spoonfuls of dough into balls with your hands. Place the dough on the greased cookie sheets.

7 Use a fork to mash them flat, first one way, then perpendicularly, to make a grid design. See photo 1.

8 Bake for 8 to 10 minutes.

9 Allow the cookies to cool before eating them.

1

What's better than peanut butter?
Peanut butter with chocolate — or more nuts!

Kiss Me
Yield: 24

Ingredients

1 batch Perfectly Peanut-Buttery dough
1 package chocolate kisses

Roll each spoonful of dough into a ball with your hands. Place the dough balls on the greased cookie sheets. Instead of flattening the dough balls with a fork, squish a chocolate candy kiss in the middle of each one. See photo 2.

Freckle Face
Yield: 24

Ingredients

1 batch Perfectly Peanut-Buttery dough
2 oz semi-sweet baking chocolate

Equipment

Grater

Grate the chocolate into the dough before you put the dough onto the greased cookie sheets. Watch your fingers! Then add extra chocolate to each cookie if you like. See photo 3.

Extra Nutty
Yield: 24

Ingredients

1 batch Perfectly Peanut-Buttery dough
1 c mixed nuts (unsalted*)

The nuts add crunch.

*If you only have salted nuts, leave the salt out of the recipe for the Perfectly Peanut-Buttery dough.

Uh-Oh–
Peanut Butter

Some people have a severe allergy to peanuts and anything made from peanuts. When sharing your homemade cookies, always tell people which ones have peanuts or peanut ingredients in them.

Heavenly Cookies

Cookies aren't exactly health food. But these great-tasting cookies don't have any extra sugar. So enjoy them anytime you want.

Applesauce Cookies

Yield: 24

Ingredients
1 c flour
1 tsp cinnamon
1 tsp baking soda
½ tsp salt
½ c your favorite nuts
1 c quick oats
   (not instant oatmeal)
1 c raisins
1 c applesauce
2 eggs
½ c vegetable oil
1 tsp vanilla extract

Equipment
Measuring cups and
   spoons
Mixing bowls
Wooden mixing spoon
   or fork
2 greased cookie sheets
Spoon

1 Preheat the oven to 375° F.

2 Mix the dry ingredients in the largest bowl. Mix the wet ingredients in the other bowl. Add the dry mixture to the wet mixture. Blend them well.

3 Spoon the dough for these drop cookies onto the greased cookie sheets.

4 Bake the dough for 8 to 10 minutes.

5 Allow the cookies to cool before eating them.

An ingredient substitution or two creates even more delicious cookies.

Coconutty Sweetness
Yield: 24

Ingredients
1 c flour
1 tsp baking soda
½ tsp salt
½ c your favorite nuts
1 c unsweetened coconut flakes
1 c chopped dates
1 c unsweetened crushed pineapple
2 eggs
½ c vegetable oil
1 tsp vanilla extract

These cookies are the kind of sweet that puts a smile on your face, but won't make your teeth hurt. I like them for breakfast or as a snack.

Gadzooks Granola
Yield: 24

Ingredients
1 c flour
1 tsp baking soda
½ tsp salt
2½ c granola
1 c applesauce
2 eggs
½ c vegetable oil
1 tsp vanilla extract

You'll like this cookie so much, you'll say, "Gadzooks! That was a good cookie!"

Yummy Oatmeal-Raisin Cookies

Chocolate and peanut butter aren't the only ingredients that make a cookie recipe delicious. Quick oats add a chewy goodness to recipes. (And you can throw in some chocolate on top, if you like.)

Original Recipe

Yield: 24

Ingredients
1 stick softened butter
⅓ c granulated sugar
⅓ c packed light brown sugar
1 egg
1 tsp vanilla extract
¾ c flour
½ tsp baking soda
¼ tsp salt
½ tsp cinnamon
¾ c quick oats (not instant oatmeal)
½ c walnut pieces
¾ c raisins

Equipment
Measuring cups and spoons
Mixing bowls
Mixer or fork
2 greased cookie sheets
Spoon

1 Preheat the oven to 375° F.

2 Cream the softened butter and sugar in a large mixing bowl.(See page 19.)

3 Add the egg and vanilla to the creamed butter and sugar. Blend the ingredients well.

4 Mix the flour, baking soda, salt, and cinnamon in the other mixing bowl. Add this dry mixture to the wet mixture. Blend it well. Add your goodies (oats, walnuts, raisins) to the dough. Mix well.

5 Spoon the dough onto the greased cookie sheets to make these drop cookies. Bake for 8 to 10 minutes.

6 Allow the cookies to cool before eating them.

Four extra-chewy cookie recipes for you!

Cinnapple
Yield: 24

Ingredients
1 stick softened butter
⅓ c granulated sugar
⅓ c packed light brown sugar
1 egg
1 tsp vanilla extract
¾ c flour
½ tsp baking soda
¼ tsp salt
1 tsp cinnamon
¾ c quick oats (not instant oatmeal)
½ c walnut pieces
1 c chopped apple

Equipment
Paring knife

Apples can be hard to chop. If you need to, get an adult to do this. One apple is enough.

Trail Mix
Yield: 24

Ingredients
1 stick softened butter
⅓ c granulated sugar
⅓ c packed light brown sugar
1 egg
1 tsp vanilla extract
¾ c flour
½ tsp baking soda
¼ tsp salt
½ tsp cinnamon
¾ c quick oats (not instant oatmeal)
1 c trail mix

Use your favorite trail mix for one-of-a-kind cookies.

My Mom's Holiday Cookies
Yield: 24

Ingredients
1 stick softened butter
⅓ c granulated sugar
⅓ c packed light brown sugar
1 egg
1 tsp vanilla extract
¾ c flour
½ tsp baking soda
¼ tsp salt
¼ tsp nutmeg
¾ c quick oats (not instant oatmeal)
⅓ c pecan pieces
⅓ c dried cranberries
½ c chocolate chips
1 T orange zest

Equipment
Grater

My mom is a fantabulous cook. Now you'll taste why! These cookies are perfect with hot apple cider on a cold day. Make orange *zest* by grating just the orange part of the peel on the smallest holes of the grater. The orange peel that comes off is called the zest. Watch your fingers!

Everything but the Kitchen Sink
Yield: 24

Ingredients
1 stick softened butter
⅓ c granulated sugar
⅓ c packed light brown sugar
1 egg
1 tsp vanilla extract
¾ c flour
½ tsp baking soda
¼ tsp salt
½ tsp cinnamon
¾ c quick oats (not instant oatmeal)
1 ¼ c goodies (to be chosen by you!)

Can't decide which goodies you want? Use them all!

So-Good Sandwiches

What could be better than a homemade cookie? TWO home-made cookies, with extra yumminess stuffed in between! That makes it a sandwich cookie. Why not ask your parents to let you eat one of these sandwiches for lunch? (It could happen.)

Ice Cream Craving
Yield: 12

Ingredients
1 batch baked cookies (pick a recipe
   from this chapter)
Ice cream (any flavor)
Chopped nuts (optional)
Mini chocolate chips (optional)

Equipment
Ice cream scoop
Butter knife

1 Set the ice cream container in the sink or on a plate while the cookies bake and cool. This lets the ice cream soften enough to work with.

2 Grab two cookies. Put a scoop of ice cream on the bottom cookie. See photo 1. Use the top cookie to mush it down until the ice cream gets to the edge.

3 You can use a knife to smooth the outside edge. For a fancy touch, roll the sides in chopped nuts or mini-chocolate chips. Repeat steps 2 and 3 for each pair of cookies.

4 Put the sandwiches in the freezer for at least 10 minutes to get the ice cream hard again. That way they won't melt all over you and your friends when you eat them.

PB&J

Yield: 12

Ingredients
1 batch baked Perfectly Peanut-Buttery
  cookies (page 68)
Jelly or jam

Equipment
Butter knife

1 Spread your favorite jelly between
two cookies. Make as many
sandwiches as you'd like.

Ultimate Peppermint Patty

Yield: 12

Ingredients
1 batch baked cookies (use one of The
  Ultimate Chocolate Cookies, pages
  66 to 67)
2 c powdered sugar
½ c vegetable shortening
1 tsp peppermint extract or oil

Equipment
Mixer or fork
Small bowl
Rubber spatula
Butter knife

1 Blend the sugar, shortening, and
extract in the bowl until the minty
filling mixture is white and fluffy.

2 Grab two cookies. Use the spatula
to spread the minty filling on top of
one cookie.

3 Press the second cookie on top of
the filling until the filling comes just
to the edges of the cookies.

4 You can clean up the edges
with the knife.

Tropical Paradise

Yield: 12

Ingredients
1 batch baked Heavenly (page 70) or
  Yummy Oatmeal-Raisin cookies
  (pages 74)
6 oz crushed pineapple
8 oz softened cream cheese

Equipment
Mixer or fork
Medium bowl
Rubber spatula
Butter knife

1 Set the cream cheese out when you
turn the oven on to bake the cookies.
(You want the cream cheese to
warm and soften.) Open the can of
pineapple and drain the juice out.

2 While the cookies are cooling, make
the filling by mixing the pineapple
with the cream cheese.

3 Grab two cookies. Use the spatula to
spread the filling on the bottom of
one cookie. (This way, the prettiest
side of the cookie will show when
the sandwich is ready.) See photo 2.

4 Press the second cookie down on
the filling so the filling just makes it
to the edges of the cookies.

5 You can use the knife to clean
up the edges. See photo 3.

Gingerrific

Gingerbread cookies wake up your taste buds with sweetness and spice any time of year. Make the basic chewy cookies, extra creamy variations, fun gingerbread people, or a sandcastle.

Goodness Gracious!

Yield: 24

Ingredients

½ stick softened butter
½ c packed light brown sugar
½ c molasses
1 tsp vanilla extract
3 ½ c flour
1 tsp baking soda
¼ tsp salt
1 T. ginger
½ tsp cinnamon
¼ tsp cloves
¼ c water

Equipment

Measuring cups and spoons
Flat surface
Waxed paper
Flour
Rolling pin
Round cookie cutters
2 greased cookie sheets

1 Preheat the oven to 375° F.

2 Cream the butter and sugar in the largest mixing bowl. (See page 19.) Add the molasses and vanilla.

3 Mix the dry ingredients together. Add them to the wet mixture. Mix well. Use the lowest speed on your mixer.

4 Mix in the water.

5 No chilling is necessary for these cutout cookies. Roll out the dough. Cut out round shapes.

6 Move the cutout dough to the greased cookie sheets. Bake for 8 to 10 minutes.

7 Allow the cookies to cool before eating them.

Tropical Treat

Yield: 24

Ingredients

1 batch Goodness Gracious! dough
Tropical Paradise sandwich filling (page 75)

Equipment

Rubber spatula

While the cookies are cooling, make a batch of the sandwich filling. Spread a creamy layer of filling on top of each cookie. Close your eyes, take a bite, and imagine that you are in Hawaii.

Lemony

Yield: 24

Ingredients

1 batch Goodness Gracious! dough
1 T lemon zest

Equipment

Grater

How do you make lemon zest? Just rub each side of a lemon against the grater. The little yellow pieces of peel that slice off are called zest. Only use the first (yellow) layer of lemon peel.

Gingerbread People

Yield: 3 or more

Ingredients
1 batch Goodness Gracious! dough
1 batch Buttercream Icing (page 26)
Food coloring

Equipment
People-shaped cutters
2 greased cookie sheets
Several small bowls
Pastry bags (page 28)

1 Preheat the oven to 375° F. Make the dough using the equipment and instructions for Goodness Gracious!

2 Wrap and chill the dough for these cutout cookies.

3 Roll out the dough. Cut out your gingerbread people.

4 Move the dough people onto the greased cookie sheets. Bake for 8 to 10 minutes.

5 While the cookies bake, mix the icing colors in the small bowls. You can pick different colors for hair, clothes, and features such as eyes, noses, and lips.

6 Allow the cookies to cool before decorating them. You can decorate the finished, cooled cookies to look like a friend who is ailing. Just use white icing to make a cast and a swathe like you see in the photo of one of my finished cookies. Call it a Get-Well-Soon cookie.

Sandcastle
Yield: 1

Ingredients
1 batch Goodness Gracious! dough (page 76)
2 batches Cookie Glue (page 27)
1 bag light brown sugar
6 ice cream cones (sugar cones)

Equipment
Pizza wheel
Pastry bags (page 28)
2 greased cookie sheets
Large serving tray

1 Making this incredible cookie will take about 4 hours. But you aren't working the whole time! Make the dough. Wrap and chill it for 20 minutes.

2 While the dough is chilling, decide what size castle you want and make a pattern for each part of your sandcastle. (I recommend pieces of no larger than 6 by 10 inches. See page 22 for pattern instructions.) A good trick is to find a box the size you want, like a shoebox, and cut it up for patterns. Build your sandcastle of out of the patterns, using tape to hold it together. Did it work? If not, make adjustments and try again until it works. If your pattern pieces won't stand up, your gingerbread sandcastle doesn't have a chance.

3 Preheat the oven to 375° F.

4 Roll out the dough about ½ inch thick. Gently press the pattern pieces into the dough and cut around the patterns.

5 Move the dough pieces to the greased cookie sheet. Bake the gingerbread for 10 to 12 minutes.

6 When you remove the cookies from the oven, allow them to set for a few minutes on the cookie sheets. Then move the gingerbread to a cooling rack. Let the gingerbread cool completely.

7 The serving tray will be your base. Assemble your sandcastle, using the Cookie Glue between all the joints. See photo 1. Don't be stingy—use a lot of Glue!

8 You'll need to prop up the sandcastle while it dries. You can use food cans or boxes. See photo 2.

9 Let your sandcastle dry for at least 3 hours before you decorate it. Then spread Cookie Glue over the whole castle and press brown sugar on it. See photo 3. This step makes the castle look as if it's made of sand. Use the same amount of sugar all over to avoid having lumps.

10 Spread the rest of the sugar on the serving platter, so it looks as if the castle is on a beach.

11 Use Cookie Glue to attach sugar to the ice cream cones. Then attach the ice cream cones upside down on the roof to create towers. Draw a door on the front of your castle using the Cookie Glue.

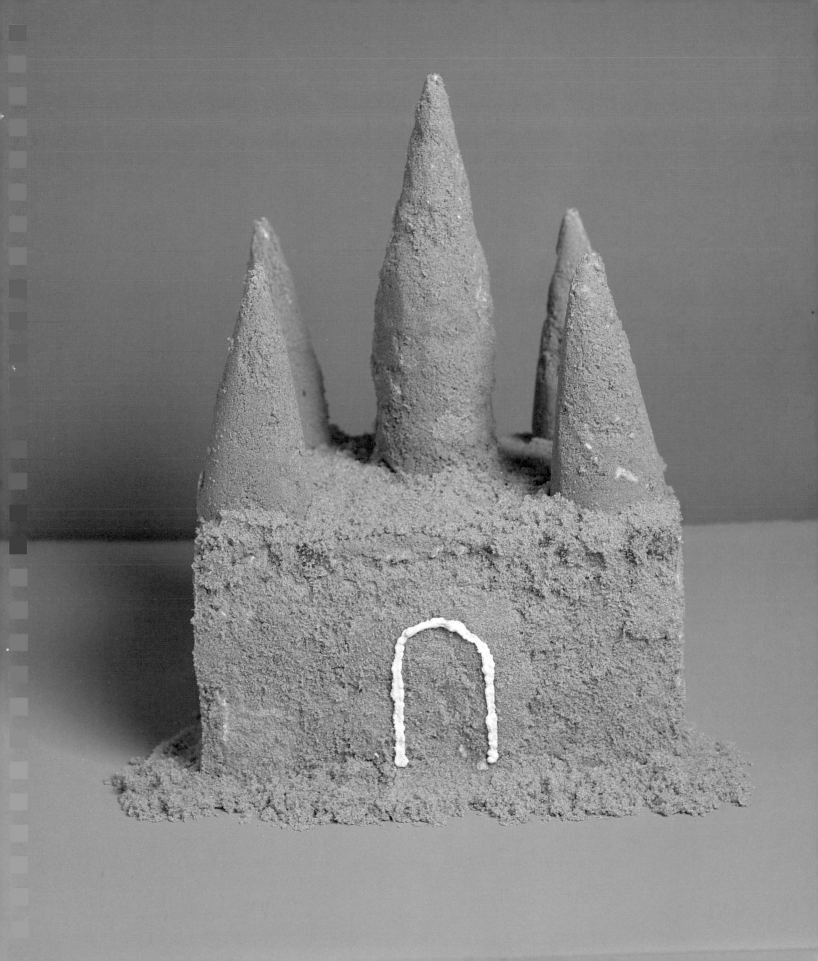

No-Bake Cookies

These are the best-tasting, grossest-looking cookies you'll ever eat. And they are easy to make. Watch out, though — the cookies are incredibly sweet.

Chocolate Chip

Yield: 24

Ingredients
1 stick butter
2 c granulated sugar
½ c milk
3 c rolled oats (not instant oatmeal)
1 c chocolate chips
1 tsp vanilla extract

Equipment
Measuring cups and spoons
Mixing bowls
Mixer, or fork and spoon
4-quart pot
Oven mitts
Wooden mixing spoon
Waxed paper

1 The method for these is totally different from regular cookies. For starters, you don't bake these cookies, so don't bother to turn on the oven. But make sure you're allowed to use the stovetop.

2 Grease the inside rim of the pot with butter. Then put the rest of the butter in the pot. See photo 1. This greasing step will prevent any boiling-over disaster.

3 Put the sugar and milk in the pot. Put the pot on the stove on medium heat. See photo 2.

4 Bring the concoction to a boil. You'll know when it's boiling. It really bubbles up! That's why you needed the big pot. See photo 3.

5 Let the concoction boil for exactly one minute, then take the pot off the heat.

6 Add the oats, chocolate chips, and vanilla. See photo 4. Stir it all up.

7 Plop spoonfuls of the mixture onto waxed paper. Be careful! Don't touch the hot dough, no matter how delicious it looks!

8 Let the cookies sit for about 20 minutes, until the cookies get hard. Simple, huh?

One of these is going to look especially gross.

Pick Your Chips
Yield: 24

1 stick butter
2 c granulated sugar
½ c milk
3 c rolled oats (not instant oatmeal)
1 tsp vanilla extract
1 c baking chips (your choice)

When you're at the grocery store, look in the section where they sell chocolate chips. There are a bazillion other kinds! Butterscotch, peanut butter, milk chocolate, white chocolate, and more. Pick one that sounds good to you.

Toss Your Cookies
(also known as Gross Out Cookies)
Yield: 24

1 stick butter
2 c granulated sugar
½ c milk
3 c rolled oats (not instant oatmeal)
1 c chocolate chips
1 tsp vanilla extract
1 package gummy worms

Dare your friends to eat these cookies! Cut the gummy worms in pieces with scissors while the cookies are cooling. Before the cookies get hard, stick gummy worms in them so it looks like worms are crawling out of muddy glops.

Cool, Cool Cookies

The cookies in this chapter don't just look cool: they are very chilled out before you bake them. How chilled out? The dough spends 2 hours to 3 days in the refrigerator. Instead of doing it all in one day, I mix and color the dough one day, and form and bake the cookies another day.

These cookies are called *millefiori* (mil-lay-fee-or-a) Millefiori is Italian for "a thousand flowers." It's a good name for them: you can make these cookies in incredible colored patterns, using as many colors as you like.

The five different recipes in this chapter all use the Sugar Cookie dough from page 31. Each recipe includes instructions for how many colors to use, how to form the dough, how to cut the dough, and how to bake it. If you are unsure about any of the baking basics, turn back to Getting Started (pages 10 to 29) for a reminder.

Spirals

Yield: 24

Ingredients

1 batch Sugar Cookie
 dough (page 31)
Food coloring
Egg Wash (page 23)

Equipment

3 bowls
Flat surface
Plastic wrap
Flour
Large knife
Pastry brush (or fingers)
2 cookie sheets

1 Divide the dough in half and make two colors of dough.

2 Wrap the doughs in plastic wrap (separately — don't mix them). Chill the dough for at least 20 minutes.

3 Shape each dough into a flat rectangle on your floured work surface. Stack one on top of the other, brushing Egg Wash between the layers. See photo 1.

4 Roll the stacked rectangles together to make a log. See photo 2.

5 Roll the log back and forth to make it smooth all around. Wrap the whole log in plastic wrap. Refrigerate the log for at least 2 hours.

6 Preheat the oven to 375°F. Grease the cookie sheets.

7 Unwrap the dough log. Carefully slice the log into cookies about ¼ inch thick. See photo 3.

8 Move the dough pieces to the greased cookie sheets. Bake the dough for 8 to 10 minutes.

9 Allow the cookies to cool before eating them.

Stripes

Yield: 24

Ingredients
1 batch Sugar Cookie dough
(page 31)
Food coloring
Egg Wash (page 23)

Equipment
3 medium size bowl
Flat surface
Plastic wrap
Large knife
Pastry brush (or fingers)
2 cookie sheets

1 Divide the dough into three equal parts. Make each section of dough a different color.

2 Shape each dough into a rectangle ¼ inch thick. Wrap the doughs in plastic (separately — don't mix them). Chill the doughs for at least 20 minutes.

3 Remove the doughs from the refrigerator and unwrap them. Stack the rectangles on top of one another, brushing Egg Wash between each layer.

4 Cut the stack in half lengthwise, and brush Egg Wash on top of each half. See photo 1.

5 Pick up one stack and place it on top of the other, to make a six-layer striped dough box.

6 Wrap the whole dough box and refrigerate it for at least 2 hours.

7 When you are ready to bake, preheat the oven to 375°F. Grease the cookie sheets.

8 Unwrap the dough log. Carefully slice the log into cookies about ¼ inch thick. See photo 2.

9 Move the dough pieces to the cookie sheets. Bake the dough for 8 to 10 minutes.

10 Allow the cookies to cool before eating them.

Checkerboard

Yield: 24

Ingredients
1 batch Sugar Cookie dough (page 31)
Food coloring
Egg Wash (page 23)

Equipment
1 medium-size bowl
Flat surface
Plastic wrap
Pastry brush (or fingers)
Flour
Large knife
2 cookie sheets

1 Follow the directions for the Stripes cookies on page 84 until you have a striped dough box.

2 Wrap and chill the "box" in the freezer for 10 minutes.

3 Slice the dough box lengthwise into three long, striped pieces. See photo 1.

4 Begin stacking these dough pieces on top of each other, brushing Egg Wash in between each layer. Make sure your layers alternate to make a checkerboard pattern. See photo 2.

5 Wrap this new checkerboard dough box and refrigerate it for at least 2 hours.

6 Preheat the oven to 375°F. Grease the cookie sheets.

7 Unwrap the dough log. Carefully slice the log into cookies about ¼ inch thick.

8 Move the dough pieces to the cookie sheets. Bake for 8 to 10 minutes.

9 Allow the cookies to cool before eating them.

Bull's-eye

Yield: 24

Ingredients

1 batch Sugar Cookie dough (page 31)
Egg Wash (page 23)
Food coloring

Equipment

3 medium size bowls
Flat surface
Plastic wrap
Flour
Large knife
Pastry brush (or fingers)
2 cookie sheets

1. Divide the dough into three sections: one large, one medium, and one small. Make each section of dough a different color.

2. Wrap the doughs in plastic wrap (separately — don't mix them). Chill the doughs for at least 20 minutes.

3. Make the large and medium batches into flat rectangles of the same size. (The medium batch will be thinner.) Stack the thinner rectangle on top of the thicker one, brushing Egg Wash in between the layers.

4. Roll the remaining section of dough into a snake as long as the rectangles. Brush it with Egg Wash and stack in on top of the rectangles. See photo 1.

5. Pinch the doughs together on one end and roll them up into a log. See photo 2. Wrap the whole log in plastic wrap, and refrigerate it for at least 2 hours.

6. When you are ready to bake, preheat the oven to 375°F. Grease the cookie sheets.

7. Unwrap the dough log. Carefully slice the log into cookies about ¼ inch thick. See photo 3.

8. Move the dough pieces to the cookie sheets. Bake for 8 to 10 minutes.

9. Allow the cookies to cool before eating them.

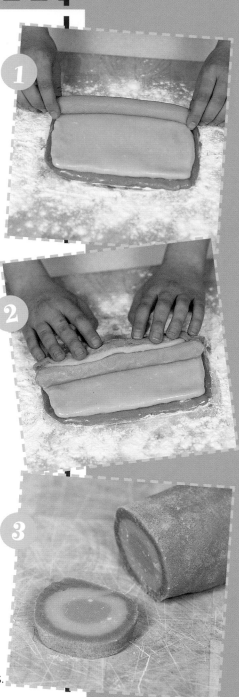

Bodacious Bouquet

Yield: 24

Ingredients
1 batch Sugar Cookie dough (page 31)
Food coloring
Egg Wash (page 23)

Equipment
3 medium size bowls
Flat surface
Plastic wrap
Flour
Large knife
Pastry brush (or fingers)
2 cookie sheets

1 Divide the dough into four batches: one large, two mediums, and one small. Color the large batch green for leaves. Make the medium batches pink and purple for petals. Make the small batch yellow for the center of the flower. Of course, you can change the colors to whatever you want.

2 Wrap each color of dough separately in plastic wrap. Put the doughs in the refrigerator for at least 20 minutes.

3 After the dough has chilled, divide the doughs that are petal color into thirds. Roll each dough into a snake. (If you are using two colors of petals, you will make six snakes.) Make them all the same length. Now roll the yellow dough into a snake the same length as the others.

4 Alternate the colors as you line up the petal snakes up on your flat, floured surface. Brush on a thin coat of Egg Wash onto each dough snake. Put the yellow snake on top of the others. See photo 1.

5 Grab all the dough snakes with both hands and roll them into one log. See photo 2. Roll the dough log a few times until it holds together.

6 Wrap up the dough log and chill it for at least 2 hours.

7 The leaves are really easy to make. Roll the green dough into a log. Mash the whole log down halfway, so that when you look at it from the end the side-view resembles an oval. Wrap and chill this dough log, too.

8 When you are ready to bake, preheat the oven to 375°F. Grease the cookie sheets.

9 Slice the chilled dough logs into cookies about ¼ inch thick. See photo 3.

10 Move the dough pieces to the cookie sheets. Bake for 8 to 10 minutes.

11 Allow the cookies to cool before eating them.

Party Down

Cookie Making Party

It's so much fun to make cookies, why not do it at a party? Use good hosting tricks to make it easier for everyone to have fun.

Hosting Tips

First, decide how many guests you'll have. If it's only two or three, you can make the cookies with them all the way from scratch. If you have more guests, it's a good idea to make the dough ahead of time and refrigerate it. At the party, have your friends help get the cookies onto the cookie sheet, bake them, and decorate them. Make sure you set up a work area before your guests arrive. Have all of the ingredients and tools ready. Fill the sink with soapy water, and make sure the dishwasher is empty if you have one. You'll be surprised by how helpful your friends are at cleaning up if you just act like it's the normal thing to do. Do you have pesky younger siblings? Remember, the reason they bug you is because they want to be just like you — they think you're the coolest person in the whole world. So be cool. Instead of leaving them out, give them a chunk of dough to play with. Little kids are also good helpers with sweeping and wiping up.

Themes

When you plan a party based around one idea, that's a theme party. Here are ideas and instructions for themes you could use.

Team Spirit

The day before your guests arrive, make Sugar Cookie dough (see page 31). Dye it with food coloring in your team's colors, and wrap and chill the dough. When your guests arrive, have them help you use this book's instructions to make cookies in the designs of Spirals, Bull's-eyes, Stripes, and Checkerboards. (See pages 83 to 87. Because you've already made and chilled the dough, start with step 3 for Spirals and Bull's-eyes).

Spring Fling

Get some cookie cutters shaped like flowers and butterflies. Your guests could cut their cookies freehand, but they might prefer to use a cutter. At the party (or ahead of time) make Lemony cookie dough using the recipe on page 76. Make icing in lots of different colors that remind you of spring. Think pink, periwinkle, yellow, bright blue, and so on. (See page 26 for my Buttercream Icing recipe). You and your friends can cut out the cookies, bake them, and then decorate.

Gingerbread People

You will need gingerbread people cookies, icing, and lots of candies to decorate with. Use the recipe on page 77 and make the gingerbread people ahead of time and you and your friends can spend all your time decorating and eating. Use the icing recipe from page 26 and pipe on faces and clothes. If you like, decorate the cookies to resemble you and your friends. Fruit leather makes cool skirts, pants, and scarves.

Slumber Party

A day before your party, make a double batch of Sugar Cookie dough using the recipe on page 31. Divide the dough. Make lots of pretty flower colors with food coloring, and color each section of dough one of the colors. Wrap and chill the dough overnight. At your party, follow the instructions for Flower Power on page 40. Everyone will have a personal bouquet.

Bling-Bling

Make any batch of cookies glittery by sprinkling granulated sugar (white sugar) on them before they go in the oven.

Giant Cookies

Giant cookies are really fun at parties. You can use any kind of cookie dough in this book. Follow the recipes on pages 91 to 92.

Pizza is great when you have a lot of friends over. The Breakfast Cookies are perfect for the morning after a slumber party. Have fun!

Pizza

Yield: 1 pie

Ingredients
1 batch Sugar Cookie dough (page 31),
 or dough of your choice
Strawberry jam
Shredded coconut
Fruit leathers

Equipment
Round pizza pan
 (not the kind with holes in it)
Spoon
Small round cutter
Pizza wheel

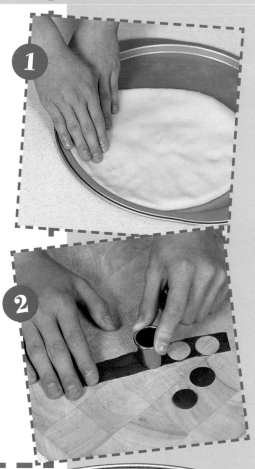

1 Preheat the oven to 375° F. Grease the pizza pan.

2 Press the dough flat in the pan. Go all the way to the edges, but don't let it get higher than the lip of the pan. See photo 1.

3 Use strawberry jam for the sauce. Bake the giant cookie at the regular temperature for the dough you have chosen, but bake it for 15 to 20 minutes. It takes longer because it's so big.

4 Allow the cookie to cool on the cookie sheet. Then sprinkle on shredded coconut for the cheese. Use a round cutter to cut out circles of fruit leather to look like pepperoni. See photo 2.

5 Slice the pizza into pieces using the pizza wheel. Eat!

Don't like fake pizza? Try this.

Super Chewy Chunky
Yield: 1 giant cookie

Ingredients
1 batch Original Recipe dough (page 72) or
 Heavenly Cookies dough (page 70)
Peanut butter (smooth or chunky)
1 handful granola

Use the equipment and baking instructions for the Pizza cookie. When it's baked, top the cookie with a layer of peanut butter and a sprinkling of granola. This is the chewiest cookie in the book!

Breakfast Cookies

Yield: 12

Ingredients
1 batch Heavenly Cookies dough
(page 70)
Your favorite jam
Freshly washed blueberries,
blackberries, or raspberries
Whipped cream
Strawberries

Equipment
2 greased cookie sheets
Spoon

1 Preheat the oven to 375° F. Grease the cookie sheets.

2 Spoon extra-large scoops of dough on to the greased cookie sheets.

3 Bake the oversized cookies at the regular temperature, but for 12 to 15 minutes.

4 Allow the cookies to cool before decorating them.

5 Spread a thin layer of jam on each cookie. Put blueberries in the jam. See photo 1.

6 Top each cookie with whipped cream and a strawberry. See photo 2.

Cookie Gifts

What's the perfect present that you can make? Cookies, of course!

Everyone loves cookies, and you get to have the fun of making them. There are lots of ways to wrap cookies up to give your gift flair. A regular glass jar looks pretty with a ribbon tied around it. You can glue buttons or paper cutouts to the jar for decoration, or you can leave it plain. To be even more fancy, line the jar with colored plastic wrap.

Colored plastic wrap is also the perfect thing to use if you're just giving a couple of cookies, like if you want to give everyone in your class a treat for Valentine's Day or Halloween. Put the cookies in the middle of a square of plastic wrap, and pull the plastic wrap straight up around them. Tie the bundle with ribbon.

If you want to send cookies in the mail to grandparents or pen pals, you should put them in tins with tight-fitting lids.

Send a Recipe

You don't even have to make cookies all the way to give a great present. You can share the joy of baking by sending most of the ingredients and all of the instructions for baking cookies.

What You Need
  Ingredients for the recipe you
        have picked
    3 resealable plastic food bags
      Permanent marker
        Jar with a lid
          Ribbons
            A card (you can make it
                from construction
                paper)
              Scissors

1 Choose a yummy recipe from this book.

2 Use a permanent marker to number the bags 1, 2, 3.

3 Measure the sugar, and put it into bag number 1.

4 Measure the flour, salt, baking powder, and any other powdery ingredients like cocoa or spices, and put them into bag number 2.

5 Measure the goodies like chocolate chips or oatmeal, and put them into bag number 3.

6 Put the bags inside the jar, and close the lid.

7 Now make the card. It should say something like this: "Here is the stuff to make The Very Best Chocolate Chip Cookies Ever. You will also need a stick of softened butter and 1 egg. Preheat the oven to 375°F. Mix the butter with the contents of bag number 1 until it's fluffy. Add the egg, and mix until it's smooth. Next, mix in the contents of bag number 2, and then mix in the goodies in bag number 3. Put spoonfuls of the dough on a greased cookie sheet, and bake it for 8 to 10 minutes. Enjoy this delicious gift with a glass of cold milk." Of course, change the card to match the kind of cookies called for in the recipe.

8 Make a hole in the corner of the card. Put the ribbon through the hole, and tie it around the jar. Make a bow from the ribbon ends.

9 Deliver your gift!

Glossary

Allergy: when a person's body can't take a certain type of food

Bake: cooking in an oven

Baking powder: a very strong dry ingredient. Don't mistake it for baking soda!

Baking rack: the wire shelf in the oven

Baking soda: a powerful dry ingredient that makes cookies puff up when they bake. The scientific term for baking soda is sodium bicarbonate.

Batch: a group of cookies. If you only have one cookie sheet, you can bake a recipe in two batches.

Beat: a way of mixing that's kind of fast and fluffs up the dough, like when you mix in eggs

Beaters: attachments for hand-held electric mixers. I like to lick the beaters after I've made icing.

Cake-decorating pastes: a very strong food coloring

Chill: putting dough in the refrigerator to cool it so it's easier to work with for cutout and Cool, Cool cookies

Cooling rack: a wire tray to cool cookies on

Cookie cutters: tools you use to stamp neat shapes out of cookie dough. I think metal cookie cutters work the best.

Cream: beating together softened butter and sugar

Culinary: about food. I went to culinary school to learn all about food.

Cutting tools: knives, pizza wheels, and cookie cutters

Cutout cookies: cool-shaped cookies made from gingerbread or sugar cookie dough

Dough: the raw mixture of ingredients that will become cookies when you bake it

Drop cookies: cookies that are made by dropping spoonfuls of dough onto a cookie sheet

Dry ingredients: ingredients that aren't wet, such as flour and salt

Eggs: oval-shaped things made by chickens

Egg white: the yellowish, clear part of the egg that isn't really white. The scientific term for egg white is albumen.

Egg yolk: the round, orangey-yellow part of the egg

Eggshell: the part of the egg you don't want to mix into your cookie dough

Electric mixer: a great tool that keeps your arm from getting too tired

Equipment: another word for tools

F: the abbreviation for Fahrenheit

Flour: powdery stuff made from wheat. Use all-purpose flour to make cookies.

Food coloring: concentrated liquid colors that you can add to icing or dough

Freestanding electric mixer: the kind of mixer pictured in this book

Grease: rubbing butter or oil on a cookie sheet so the cookies won't stick to it

Handheld electric mixer: just what it sounds like

Ingredients: all the different foods that go into a recipe

Jimmies: sprinkles shaped like tiny cylinders

Metal spatula: a flat utensil with a handle

mL: abbreviation for milliliters

Oz: abbreviation for ounce or ounces. 2 T = 1 oz and 8 oz = 1 cup

Packed: when an ingredient is squished down into the measuring cup

Paddle attachment: the triangular part for a freestanding electric mixer that you use to make dough and icing

Paring knife: a little sharp knife that's good for tiny precise cuts

Pastry bag: a bag you put icing in to decorate cookies

Pastry brush: a paint brush for food

Piping: decorating cookies by drawing on them with icing from a pastry bag

Pizza wheel: a round cutting tool with a handle

Preheat: letting the oven heat to the right temperature for baking. Some ovens have a "Preheat" setting, but with most you just turn on "Bake."

Recipe: a plan for making something delicious

Rolling pin: a tool for flattening dough

Rubber spatula: a spreading utensil

Salmonella: invisible bacteria in raw eggs that can make you sick

Separating eggs: getting the yolk and white apart

Softened: warmed to room temperature

Spooning the dough: getting spoonfuls of dough to make drop cookies

Substitution: using a different ingredient

Tablespoon: a measurement that equals ½ oz or 3 tsp

T: abbreviation for tablespoon

tsp: abbreviation for teaspoon

Teaspoon: a measurement that equals ⅓ T

Timer: a tool that helps you remember when to take your cookies out of the oven

Utensils: small kitchen tools with handles, such as spoons and spatulas

Vanilla extract: a yummy flavoring that's made from the seeds of a flowering plant called an orchid

Volume: how much space something takes up

Wet ingredients: ingredients that aren't dry, such as eggs and milk

Whip: to mix very fast to make a concoction super-fluffy, such as icing

Whisk attachment: the part you add a stand up mixer to whip

Yield: how many cookies a recipe makes. Depending on how big you make your cookies, your yield might be a little bit different from mine.

Zest: the colored part of the peel of a citrus fruit such as an orange or lemon. Zest has a very strong flavor that only tastes good when it's mixed with other ingredients.

Acknowledgments

Infinite love and thanks to my sweet husband, Stevie D., for his unfailing support, and for taking on the grueling task of tasting so many cookies.

A great big shout out to my enormous family — y'all are my heart!

Thanks to Veronika and Joe, wonderful people to work with.

Thanks to Stacey and Rain, too. Stacey, you made the book so beautiful.

Thanks to our models

Weston	Isaac
Rabb Scott	Gus
Olivia	Barcley
Noah	Bailey
Marcus	Anna
Mali	Alex
Lillian	A.J.
Lacey	

Metrics

Need to convert the measurements in this book to metrics? Here's how:

- To convert degrees Fahrenheit to degrees Celsius, subtract 32 and then multiply by .56.
- To convert inches to centimeters, multiply by 2.5.
- To convert ounces to grams, multiply by 28.
- To convert teaspoons to milliliters, multiply by 5.
- To convert tablespoons to milliliters, multiply by 15.
- To convert cups to liters, multiply by .24.

Index

Acknowledgments, 95

Allergy, 69

Animals, cookies shaped like, 32, 34, 52, 56, 60

Baking instructions, 24-25

Chilling the dough, 21

Chocolate, cookies made with, 44, 45, 64, 65, 66, 67, 69, 73, 75, 80, 81

Constructing one-of-a-kind shapes, 23

Cookie cutters, 22

Cookie Glue, 27

Cooling cookies, 25

Cream, 20

Cutout cookies, kinds of, 30-48, 52-60, 76-78, making, 21-22

Cutters. *See* Cookie cutters

Cutting the dough, 22

Decorating cookies, 26-29

Dedication, 5

Dog treats, 61

Drop cookies, kinds of, 64-73, 80-81, 92, making, 20

Egg Wash, 23

Equipment, 12-13

Food coloring, cookies dyed with, 36, 40, 45, 83, 84, 85, 86

Freezing cookie dough, 25

Fruit, cookies made with, 50, 73, 75, 76, 92

Get-Well-Soon cookie, 77

Giant cookies, 90-92

Gifts, giving cookies as, 93

Gingerbread cookies, 76-78

Glossary, 94

Greasing a cookie sheet, 20

Gross-looking cookies, 80-81

Icing, 26-27

Jelly, cookies made with, 48, 29, 50, 67, 75, 91

Low-sugar cookies, 70-71

Measuring, 16-17

Metrics, 95

Mixing, 18-19

Nuts, cookies made with, 65, 67, 68, 69, 71, 72, 73, 75, 91

Party ideas, 88-90

Pastry bag, 28

Peeking in the oven, 24

Piping, 28

Preheat, 19

Recipe, reading a, 14

Refrigerator cookies, 82-87

Rolling the dough, 21

Safety tips, 11

Salmonella, 23

Seasonal cookies, 32, 34, 38, 40, 42, 45, 48, 53, 58, 59, 73

Separating eggs, 27

Softening butter, 18

Spooning the dough, 20

Storing cookies, 25

Substitutions, 14

Table of contents, 6-7

Timing, 24

Tools. *See* Equipment

Yield, 14